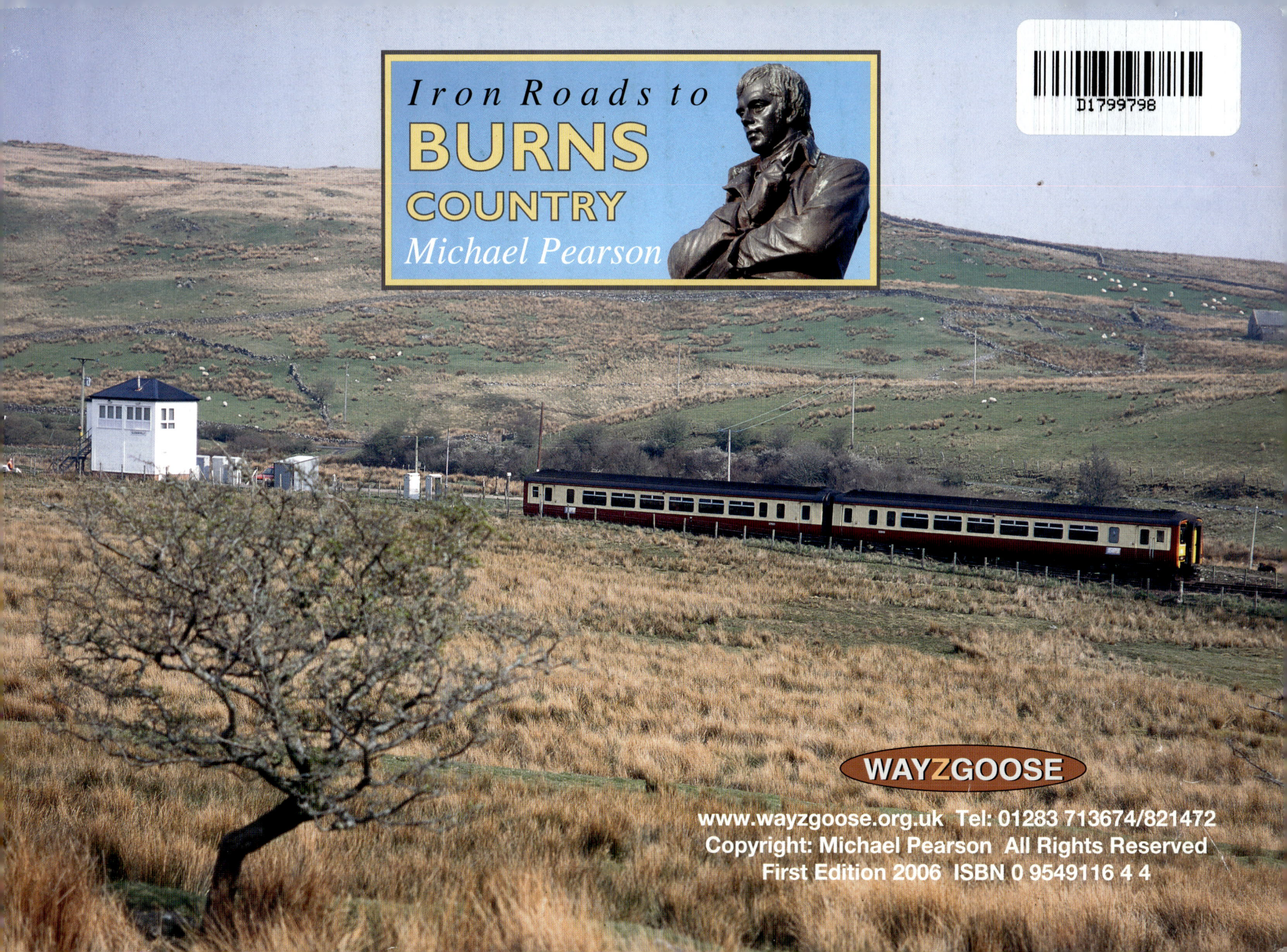

Iron Roads to
BURNS
COUNTRY
Michael Pearson

WAY**Z**GOOSE

www.wayzgoose.org.uk Tel: 01283 713674/821472
First Edition 2006 ISBN 0 9549116 4 4

MY parents met for the first time on VJ night and, I daresay, provided their own personal fireworks in addition to those being lit on the Lawe Top that evening: eight days after Hiroshima, these, after all, were kindly explosions on a human scale. NAAFI-dancing their way around the strict mores of South Shields society, they were married nine weeks later on 22nd October 1945. After an of necessity austere reception, my paternal grandfather gave them a lift by car to Dumfries. One might intrude on them, phut-phutting through the Tyne Gap under the shadow of Hadrian's Wall in a war-weary, woe-begone Morris; shadowy connections in the motor trade providing my grandfather with sufficient quantities of strictly rationed fuel. From Dumfries - infuriatingly oblivious to railway subtleties, let alone Burns - they caught a train to Kilmarnock, changing there for Ayr, their honeymoon destination. For my Scots father this represented a 'hamecoming' to nostalgically cherished childhood roots. My English mother was less enamoured: freshly post-war, Ayr was not at its most demure. For public consumption, the highlight of their holiday was a visit to a Music Hall. But by and large money was tight, and there were few luxuries to be had on a sergeant's pay.

*   *   *

Just as Northern France is shunned by those in a rush to reach the Dordogne, the landscapes of south-west Scotland are traditionally brushed aside by those in a hurry to get to the Highlands. There are still great tracts of emptiness to be found in this reticent part of the world; a point quickly grasped by Richard Hannay at the outset of his adventures in John Buchan's *The Thirty-Nine Steps*: 'Then I got out an atlas (and) fixed on Galloway as the best place to go. It was the nearest wild part of Scotland - and from the look of the map was not over thick with population - a train left St Pancras at 7.10, which would land me at any Galloway station in the late afternoon'. Mining engineers disguised as milkman have to head for Euston nowadays if they are to elude the police and foreign powers. A Virgin Pendolino will have you up in Carlisle in no time at all, but you will not find it easy to leap from the train at a providential signal stop.

Buchan aside, the literary landscapes featured in these pages are inextricably linked with Scotland's national poet, Robert Burns. His bonny Nithsdale was still more than a half century short of having a railway laid through it. Yet one imagines Burns would not have subscribed to Wordsworth's antipathy towards such an advent. From his famously egalitarian stance he is far more likely to have welcomed it as a begetter of opportunity and an improver of man's lot; whilst the additional prospect of encountering 'sonsie' lasses within the confines of the four infinitely companion-able and discrete walls of a carriage comp-artment would have greatly appealed to his muse:

Hail awesome beastie on yon parallel gleamin' rails
A' doon Nithsdale thy whistle wails
Thy muckle ferrus belly fu o' fire and water
Yet sonsie as ony o' Sanquhar's daughters
Oh fain I would wi' thee gang rovin
Doon to Dumfries in the gloamin.

Fair as ony; aye an fit an fettle
Steamin laik yon copper kettle
Spewin cluds frae thy reekin lum
Makin mair clatter than ony weaver's loom
An wi a couthie lassie dangled on ma lap,
Gang we wad in glory an conquer Polquhap!

Sadly, the Glasgow & South Western Railway - who operated most of the routes covered by this guide prior to the grouping of the railways in 1923 - did not see fit to mimic the North British Railway's mining of Sir Walter Scott's rich vein of inspiration in the naming of their locomtive fleet. To match the memorable likes of *Laird o'Monkbarns*, *Cuddie Headrigg*, *Peter Poundtext* and *Luckie Mucklebackit*, we might have had equally romantic Burnsian nomenclature such as *Poosie Nansie*, *Collection Mitchell*, *Lovely Davies*, and, of course, *Tam o' Shanter*; why, even darker names like *The Wounded Hare* or *Despondency* might have graced splashers with a dry sense of Scotch wit. It was left to the diesel age for *The Lass o' Ballochmyle* to be celebrated successively by 37694, 37692 and 47635. In fact the Sou' Western, as it was affectionately known, hardly went in for naming at all. And even more regrettably the indigenous designs of its resident mechanical engineers - the Stirlings, Smellie, Manson, Drummond and Whitelegg - went quickly to the breaker's torch under the merciless yoke of LMS standardisation policy. Even Robert Whitelegg's late sextet of massive Baltic 4-6-4 tank locomotives - designed primarily for the Clyde coast expresses but also used between Glasgow and Carlisle - were rendered redundant after barely a dozen years in traffic.

The Glasgow & South Western was the third largest railway company in Scotland. A fiercely proud concern, it enjoyed (or, more accurately, 'endured') a particularly intense rivalry with the Caledonian Railway; especially in the coalfields and in competition for the Clyde Coast traffics. The great railway historian, C. Hamilton Ellis, pithily described the two concerns as being 'usually at point of dirk'. In association with the Midland Railway the G&SWR provided an alternative means of getting from Glasgow to London via Leeds and Leicester. And if this partnership could not compete with the schedule offered by the Caledonian and London & North Western railways via Crewe, the sumptuous rolling stock of the slower route and its scenic charms were a powerful inducement to the travelling public: a colourful Land o' Burns poster produced collaboratively by the Midland and Sou' Western implied that poetry and romance were guaranteed accompaniments to journeys on their route.

My newly-wed parents were too late to enjoy the Glasgow & South Western in its independent glory, and by

the time I was being wheeled in my pram down cobbled, tram-lined streets to Paisley Canal, even the LMS was a thing of the past. According to family lore, I was bewitched by the trains; a seduction that has never departed. But it was a budding relationship short-changed by sudden emigration south of the border. Only through subsequent childhood holidays was I gradually reacquainted with the lost empires of the G&SWR. No compunction was required of Great Uncle George in abandoning me by the lineside while he played bowls on the Garthland Lane Rink. This was better than *Z Cars*, Tottenham Hotspur and *The Victor* all rolled into one. To the unpractised eye the frequent procession of trains looked all alike; big black tank locomotives coupled to long rakes of maroon coloured carriages. But, informed by my *Ian Allan ABC*, I was soon discerning enough to distinguish the Fairburn engines which commenced with a '4', from the Riddles engines, whose numbers began with an '8'. And perhaps it was there that a love was kindled for the very shape of numbers every bit as keen as the appreciation, that was to come later, of certain shapes of calf, certain arches of eyebrow, and certain declivities of *decolletage*.

Further encounters slowly accrued, many of them already recounted in *Railway Holiday in Scotland*. However, my first remembered journey over the Sou' Western main line was southwards out of Kilmarnock in 1968, behind a 'Peak' on a slackly scheduled Sunday journey, which involved wrong-line running east of Annan - and much waving of flags by pilot-men with armbands - in the days when that stretch of line was still double-tracked. Beneath the big red facade of Johnnie Walker's bottling plant my father saw me off on what might well have been the first occasion that he found himself back on Kilmarnock station since his honeymoon; though, with typical reticence, he didn't mention that to me. Following sixty years later in my parents post-nuptial footsteps, I can only be grateful for their chance encounter at the end of the war on the banks of the Tyne; and thankful too that there are still Iron Roads to Burns Country for their train-besotted only child to explore.

Carlisle

Using This Guide

Twenty-five 'one inch to one mile' maps portray the course of the lines covered within. Each map is accompanied by a running commentary on matters historical, topographical, and related to railway operation past and present. A Gazetteer section gives details of the majority of places served by rail, offering a pithy 'pen portrait' together (as appropriate) with lists of places to seek refreshment and find accommodation, details of shops and places to visit, tourist information and connecting forms of public transport. Where accuracy is essential when planning an itinerary, you are urged to contact the telephone number or website quoted for up to date details.

Scheduled Services

Day to day services on the lines covered by this guide are exclusively provided by First ScotRail. With the exception of the electrified 'outer suburban' routes from Glasgow to Ayr and Largs, current service patterns are irregular, but there are 'roughly' seven through trains between Carlisle and Glasgow via Dumfries (three of which originate from Newcastle); two through trains between Carlisle and Stranraer (both of which originate from Newcastle); and five through trains between Glasgow and Stranraer. There are additionally a number of short workings between Carlisle and Dumfries; Kilmarnock and Ayr or Girvan; and Kilmarnock and Glasgow that pad out the timetable. All these services are operated by Class 156 diesel units.

Tickets & Travelcards

The following stations covered in this guide are staffed and have booking offices selling tickets and dispensing information: Carlisle, Dumfries, Kilmarnock, Glasgow Central, Paisley Gilmour Street, Kilwinning, Irvine, Prestwick International Airport, Prestwick Town, Troon, Ayr, Girvan, Stranraer; Saltcoats, Ardrossan South

Beach and Largs. Additionally many suburban stations within the SPT network but not featured in the Gazetteer (for example Barrhead) are also staffed. Where no booking office is on site, tickets may be purchased on the train. Tickets in advance for First ScotRail services can be booked at principal staffed stations throughout the United Kingdom, through rail appointed Travel Agents, on line at *www.firstscotrail.com* or by telephoning First ScotRail telesales on 08457 55 00 33.

Charter Trains

Unaccountably, few charter trains traverse the lines featured in this guide. A notable exception are the tours operated by the Scottish Railway Preservation Society who can be contacted by visiting their website *www.srps.org.uk* or by telephoning 01698 263814.

Bicycles

Bicycles are conveyed free of charge on First ScotRail services. The Class 156 diesel units can convey up to six bicycles per two car unit. Reservations are compulsory between Carlisle and Glasgow and Stranraer and should be made at principal staffed stations of First ScotRail Telesales on 08457 55 00 33 up to eight weeks in advance but no later than two hours before the train *commences* its journey. Between Glasgow and Paisley, Ayr and Largs you may take your bicycle without prior reservation subject to space being available.

Reading

Ayrshire & Renfrewshire's Lost Railways by Gordon Stansfield. Stenlake ISBN 1 84033 077 5
Branches & Byways - Southwest Scotland and the Border Counties by Robert Robotham. Oxford Publishing Co. ISBN 0 86093 5752

Burns Country by David Carroll. Sutton ISBN 0 7509 2213 3
Burns Lore of Dumfries & Galloway by James A. Mackay. Alloway Publishing ISBN 0 907526 36 5
The Complete Illustrated Poems, Songs & Ballads of Robert Burns. Lomond Books ISBN1 85152 018 X
An Illustrated History of Carlisle's Railways by W. A. C. Smith and Paul Anderson. Irwell Press ISBN 1 871608 73 2
An Illustrated History of Glasgow's Railways by W. A. C. Smith and Paul Anderson. Irwell Press ISBN 1 871608 33 3
Mining - Ayrshire's Lost Industry by Guthrie Hutton. Stenlake ISBN 1 872074 88 X
Dumfries & Galloway - An Illustrated Architectural Guide - John R. Hume. The Rutland Press ISBN 1 873190 34 4
LMS Engine Sheds Volume Seven by Chris Hawkins etc. Irwell Press ISBN 1 871 608 10 4
The Girvan & Portpatrick Junction Railway by C. E. J. Fryer. The Oakwood Press ISBN 0 85361 448 2
Additional books of further interest are included within the text.

Useful Contacts

The Glasgow & South Western Railway Association are an enthusiastic group devoted to the memory of the railway company which so faithfully served south-west Scotland until 1923. Further details from their website: *www.gswra.org.uk*

Douglas Blades specialises in transport books and can be contacted by email: *sales@douglasblades.sol.co.uk*

ACoRP - Association of Community Rail Partnerships. Tel: 01484 847790 *www.acorp.uk.com* Promotional group for rural and local railways supported by the DfT, ATOC and sponsored by local government and the rail industry.

Acknowledgements

The author and publisher are extremely grateful to the following bodies and individuals who contributed to this book: Les Byers of Ellisland, Geoffrey Evison of Berwick-on-Tweed, Charles Jencks of Portrack, Robert Martin of Sanquhar, Roland Paxton of Heriot-Watt University, Dave Pratt of the Glasgow & South Western Railway Association and John Yellowlees of First ScotRail.

The illustrations on pages 2 and 3 are by Eric Leslie, whilst the photographs on pages 5 and 9 are by Robert Armitstead. Travel facilities were kindly provided by First ScotRail and Virgin Trains. Special thanks to Karen Tanguy of Wayzgoose and Hawksworths of Uttoxeter.

Stop Press

Reliable sources suggest that the display screens at Kilmarnock have been revived, and the pre-recorded train-announcing lassie is being instructed phonetically on the pronounciation of Kilwinning.

Carlisle Annan Dumfries
KILMARNOCK GLASGOW

Robert Armitstead

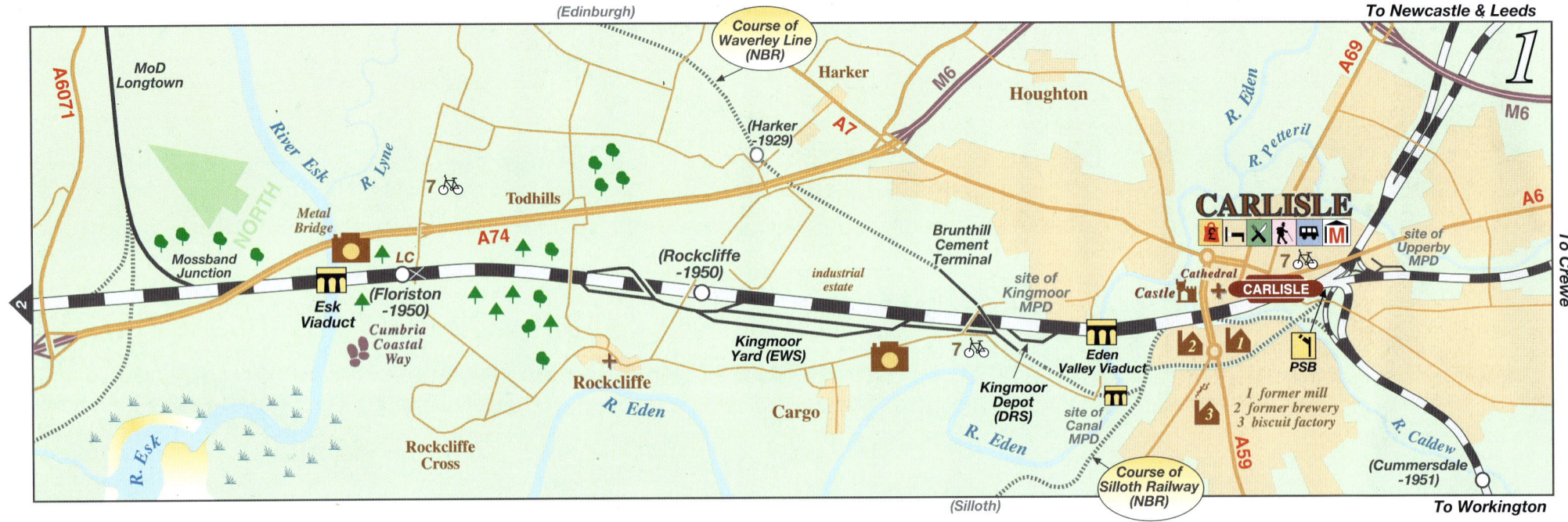

THERE are two ways of reaching Glasgow from Carlisle by train. You can charge over Beattock on the old Caledonian Railway route aboard an all-singing, all-dancing, all-tilting *Super Voyager* or *Pendolino*, gobbling up the hundred and two miles in eighty minutes. Or you can follow the former Glasgow & South Western line via Dumfries and Kilmarnock, just a dozen or so miles longer, but taking almost twice as long over the journey in what British Rail once sportingly termed a *Sprinter* unit. Back in the Golden Age of trains, with Pre-grouping rivalry and pride at stake, the difference was less apparent: in 1910 the Caledonian's 3.55pm express from Carlisle reached Glasgow Central at 6.15pm; departing seven minutes later, the Sou' Western could get you to St Enoch by 6.35pm!

By definition, the *Iron Roads* guides cater for the discerning traveller, the man (or, significantly, often the woman) with time at their disposal to absorb the nuances of landscape and social history disdained by the hurrying masses. Such individuals can afford to linger over the Frostian routes 'less travelled by', the carriage window a street theatre guaranteed to parade the sublime and absurd in equal measure.

Sir William Tite's handsome 'Citadel' station of 1847 takes its architectural cue from Carlisle's adjacent Law Courts, designed by Sir Robert Smirke almost fifty years earlier. Smirke's Citadel, modelled on Henry VIII's, consists of a pair of redbrick, battlemented, cylindrical towers. Tite's railway station frontage echoes the Tudor characteristics of its neighbour a stone's throw across Court Square. Inside, a cathedral hush descends between trains and it is easy to become lost in admiration of the architecture, however impatiently you may be anticipating your departure.

But depart you must, and from its outset the journey repays concentration. On one side a cathedral and a castle, on the other a high chimnied textile mill, a brewery converted into housing, and a biscuit factory jostle for your attention as the train accelerates over pointwork before crossing the Eden Valley Viaduct and extracting itself from the city centre. Downstream, the viaduct which used to carry the Waverley Route to Edinburgh remains resolutely intact.

In steam days Kingmoor Motive Power Depot lay alongside the up side of the line. The Caledonian Railway built it in 1873 and it saw use for ninety-four years. During the twilight years of steam it was known for its allocation of Britannia and Clan class Pacifics. The site is sapling and silver birch-covered wasteground now and those more passionate about diesel traction will be watching through the windows on the opposite side of train to see what locomotives are on display at the DRS depot of the same name. Direct Rail Services began life exclusively providing haulage for British Nuclear Fuels, but in recent years they have widened their activities, notably forming a close relationship with the road haulier W. H. Malcolm, for whom they operate flagship intermodal services along the West Coast Main Line between Grangemouth and Daventry at much greater speeds than can be managed by motorway. Their fleet's distinctive blue livery is one of the most handsome on the railway network, and even the briefest of glimpses from the train is likely to reveal examples of classes 20, 37, 47 and 66.

Just beyond DRS's premises an overbridge carries a remaining stub of the fabled Waverley Route across the line. It was closed amidst much controversey and acrimony in 1969, a hundred and seven years after the first train, operated by the North British Railway, had made a through journey between Edinburgh and Carlisle via Hawick. It was a romantic line, traversing dramatic scenery and beloved of railway enthusiasts who still get goose-pimples at the thought of travelling behind a Gresley Pacific over Whitrope summit. Recent proposals to have the southern end of it re-opened for the extraction of timber from Kielder Forest have as yet not materialised, but the northern section between Edinburgh and Galashiels is to be re-opened as a commuter route. Incidentally, the stub at this end has been retained to serve a cement depot, whilst at Riccarton Junction, where the Waverley Route once connected with a line from Hexham in the remotest of circumstances, a devoted group of 'Friends' are painstakingly bringing a thin sliver of the old railway back to life.

In its heyday, Carlisle was served by no less than seven different railway companies who each jealously operated their own installations and infrastructure. Even at the beginning of the nineteen-sixties, nine different goods yards still functioned labour-intensively. Prior to Beeching, the London Midland Region of British Railways came up with a scheme to rationalise freight operations by the provision of one massive marshalling yard. They laid seventy-two miles of reception, recessing, sorting and departure sidings on four hundred and eighty acres of land at Kingmoor. Automated hump shunting techniques allowed wagons to roll into their required lines by gravity. It cost four and a half million pounds - call it a billion now - but they reckoned the savings made would pay for it in ten years. It's a cruel world where economists are no better than soothsayers, within ten years this magnificent, state of the art marshalling yard was all but obsolete. Your first sight of it now is a derelict control tower. Once this was linked by radio-telephones with the drivers of the diesel shunting locomotives, now it looks like something left over from a world war two aerodrome. You begin to suspect the worse, but there has been a melodramatic twist to this particular railway tale, for, in place of ruin and decay, Kingmoor Yard has been reinvented by EWS, Britain's largest rail freight operator, as a busy hub for a wide range of traffics.

The crow-stepped station building at ROCKCLIFFE is still intact, despite having been closed over half a century ago. FLORISTON suffered a worse fate, for it was demolished entirely. Here the quadruple track pairs down to double and the train emerges from woodland to cross the River Esk as it makes its way out into the Solway Firth. Mossband Junction provides access to a Ministry of Defence depot at Longtown. A long vanished North to East chord once enabled through workings to and from the Waverley Line. An old engine shed, which looks as if it has seen agricultural use, is virtually the only clue to the existence of yet another abandoned line, one which passed beneath the main line to provide a link with the First World War munitions factories which occupied much of the neighbourhood.

Esk Viaduct

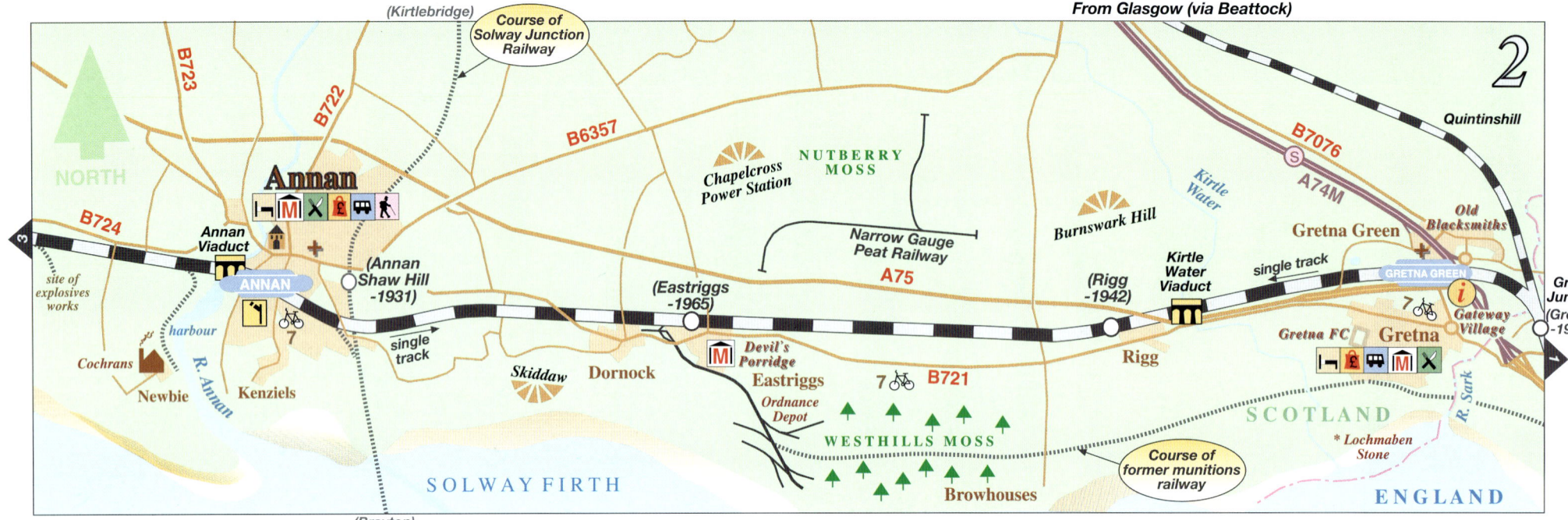

GRETNA'S 'crow-stepped' railway station is still intact. In the heyday of the village's marriage trade ministers used to meet the trains touting for business. Crossing the Sark, you leave England and its Burnsian 'Parcel of Rogues' behind you. A sharply curved cutting, through which the train beats out a rallentando rhythm on jointed track, leads to a singling of the line and the station at GRETNA GREEN, closed in 1965 but re-opened twenty-eight years later. Whether you are alighting or eloping the rebirth of Gretna Green as a railhead has at least provided this far corner of Dumfries & Galloway with an alternative for commuters to the slow, turgid drive into Carlisle.

Sarkfoot, where the river runs out into the firth, marked the easternmost extremity of Robert Burns territory as an exciseman. In 1792 he played a small part in the daring capture of the smuggler's brig *Rosamond* here. A greyhound stadium catches the eye as the train leaves Gretna. There is also a thriving football club here, now making good progress through the Scottish leagues after years playing inappropriately across the River Sark as a non-league club in another country. Founded in 1946, the 'Black & Whites' played their first season in the Dumfriesshire Amateur League before emigrating south.

With the unforseen growth in coal traffic over the Nith Valley Line, railway operators have had cause to regret the precipitate singling of the Gretna to Annan section in 1974. Redoubling is an acknowledged necessity, but if and when the budget will permit this, is less clear. There has been a ninefold increase in coal moving over the border in five years, a small matter of nine million tonnes being predicted for 2005. There are two sources for this traffic: Hunterston on the Firth of Clyde (Map 25) which receives imported coal; and Ayrshire where coal continues to be mined by opencast means.

During the First World War another railway ran more or less parallel to the Glasgow & South Western line. It was laid to provide access to the munitions works which lined the banks of the Solway Firth for nine miles between Longtown and Dornock. They had been established here in 1916 in response to a very real need for increased stocks of ammunition required on the battlefields of France. At the height of their activity the works employed over thirty thousand workers, a large proportion of them women, who were celebrated in a patriotic ditty called *The Gretna Girls*: 'Girls from Scottish hillsides, strong in health and vigour, girls from desk and counter, neat in style and figure' - Burns would have been beside himself! Nearly fifty miles of standard gauge lines and sidings were constructed to serve the munitions plants, and there was an equally large system of narrow gauge lines. Passenger services were operated to ferry the workforce and goods to bring in raw material and take the finished munitions out. Drunkeness was an unforseen by-product of all this activity - Lloyd George maintained that alcohol abuse was more detrimental to the war effort than the German submarine fleet. A State Management Scheme was introduced in the area to limit the sale of alcohol, its effect was still being felt in Carlisle fifty years later! After the war the sites were cleared and astonishingly little remains apart from a rail-linked Ministry of Defence estabalishment at Eastriggs.

Unsurprisingly, much of the line runs on the level and wide views are obtainable through the train window: southwards over Solway Firth to a horizon bounded by the Lake District, notably Skiddaw; and northwards where the dominant landmarks are the four cooling towers of the decommissioned nuclear power station at Chaplecross, and the distinctively shaped summit of an ancient hill fort on

Burnswark Hill. In a manner more reminiscent of Ireland than Scotland, a narrow gauge railway is employed in the extraction of peat from Nutberry Moss.

The astonishing Solway Junction Railway once bridged the firth between Annan and Bowness on the English side. It was opened in 1869, predominantly to carry Cumberland ore to Lanarkshire's ironworks, but the bottom had fallen out of that particular market within a few short years. A rather desultory passenger service plied between Kirtlebridge on the Caledonian main line and Brayton on the Maryport & Carlisle Railway, but even this was interrupted when the bridge across the Solway was damaged by ice floes in the arctic winter of 1881. Three years elapsed before trains were able to steam across the firth again. There was a surge of traffic during the First World War, but the line closed permanently in 1921. The bridge, however, was not demolished until 1935, enabling it to be used surreptitiously for a number of years by local pedestrians. Over a mile long, it must have been a nerve-wracking hike, though one of particular value to Scots anxious to escape the confines of a liquor-free Sabbath. A shuttle service of passenger trains remained in operation between Annan Shaw Hill and Kirtlebridge until 1931. Stone parapets, spanned solely by a waste pipe now, mark the point at which the SJR crossed the G&SWR main line.

The train slows for ANNAN as the line redoubles and you pass the playing fields of a handsome academy typical of the town's fine red sandstone architecture. The railway station doesn't let the side down either. It dates from 1848 and has a sense of permanence about it, even though it is now unstaffed and host to a bar. A substantial canopy protects Carlisle-bound passengers from the worst of the Solway Firth's frequent rain squalls, whilst the platform on the opposite side is overlooked by a timber built signal box of a Glasgow & South Western style which you will grow more familiar with as the journey unfolds. The down line is bi-directional and can thus, for example, be used to overtake up coal trains.

A fine brace of sandstone viaducts ushers the line westwards over rooftops and across the River Annan. A fish processing factory emphasises that the town still provides a living for a small fishing fleet. Fishing for salmon with traditional haaf nets is another means of making ends meet hereabouts, but it is a long time since Annan was recognised as a centre for ship-building. Whammel boats evolved as an indigenous design for drift netting in the Solway Firth.

Diverted Virgin Voyager near Annan

Robert Armitstead

The river winds for a further mile downstream before issuing into the firth. En route it is overlooked by Cochran's massive boiler works, established here at the end of the 19th century. Previously Cochrans had been ship-builders in Birkenhead. A branch ran down off the main line to serve the works, and there was a workmen's halt at Newbie Junction. As the railway continues towards Dumfries, it passes the site of an explosive works at Powfoot dating from the Second World War. At its busiest four thousand people were employed at the plant. Now simply a lattice-framed signal post, a rusty lever-frame, and a faint scar in a neighbouring field shows where a branch curved into the works which also supported an internal narrow gauge system.

Criffel and the Nith estuary

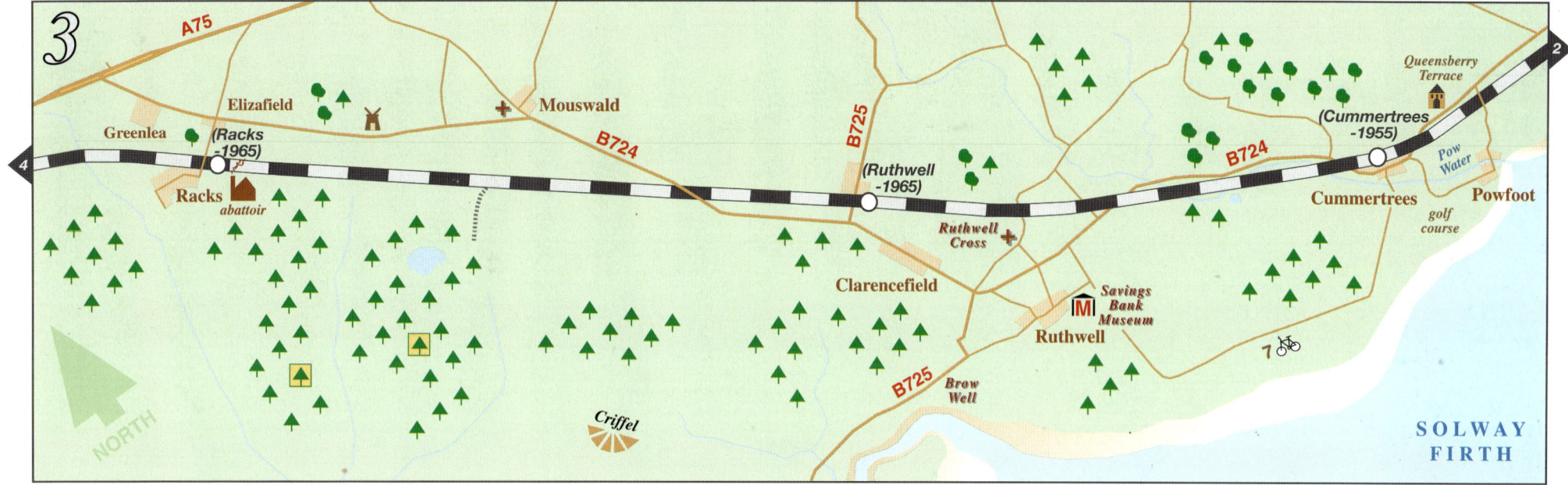

CUMMERTREES, Ruthwell and Racks may sound like some doughty pre-war forward line for Dumfries's famous football team, Queen of the South - all knee-length shorts, hobnail boots and toothless grins - but the truth of the matter is that they are a trio of abandoned stations between Annan and Dumfries. CUMMERTREES might have enjoyed a more glittering history if the seaside development dreamt of by General Brook of Kinmount, a large estate lying to the north of the railway, had ever taken off. A stillborn legacy of this misplaced aspiration overlooks the railway in the elaborate shape of Queensberry Terrace, a flamboyant Arts & Crafts row of houses which look as though they have escaped from Lytham St Annes. It was envisaged that neighbouring Powfoot would be also absorbed by this development, but it remains a soporific Solway-side village, notable solely for its golf course, designed by James Braid, which dates from 1903.

The low-lying landscape, together with an abundance of track-side gorse and sheep-filled pastures evokes a subjective symmetry with the railway which runs across Anglesey. Over on the far side of the Solway, Skiddaw becomes a doppleganger for Snowdon as glimpsed beyond the Menai Strait. Though hardly in the same league in terms of height, Criffel at 1866ft becomes the dominant peak on the western horizon. The lie of the land plays tricks with your sense of distance. Those transmitting masts, for example, which appear firmly rooted on the Scottish shore are at Anthorn in Cumbria.

At RUTHWELL the platforms are still intact, as is the big sandstone station house, in good repair for use as a domestic dwelling. Cast-iron signposts on neighbouring by-roads still point deceptively to 'Ruthwell Station' as if forty years of trains not calling here is an historic irrelevance, as if Beeching was an aberration, a bad dream in poor taste. Perhaps, after all, you can still alight here and walk down scented lanes to pay homage to the extraordinary Ruthwell Cross secreted for safe keeping within the parish kirk, a mere thirteen centuries after it was hewn and carved. Or continue to the village itself - the almost obligatory pair of miles away from the station which claims to serve it - and here stumble upon a shrine to the Reverend Henry Duncan who saved the cross, and who, with a Scots sense of sound financial husbandry, founded the concept of Savings Banks. Duncan also met Burns as a boy and played a leading role in the erection of the poet's Mausoleum at Dumfries in 1817. A mile west of Ruthwell, Brow Well is a chalybeate spring. Burns spent the last three weeks of his life nearby in 1796, phlegmatically taking the waters on his physician's advice and bathing in the freezing firth, an inappropriate cure if ever there was one. Pigs, by the way, were first introduced to Scotland in the vicinity of Ruthwell in 1760.

The line climbs at 1 in 200 through Ruthwell before descending at 1 in 150 towards Racks. Mouswald never qualified for a station, but it has a pretty little parish church and a large cluster of farm buildings dominated by the tapered tower of an old windmill with a conical cap. No station, but old maps depict sidings on the down side of the line, and a short branch line leading into the wastes of Lochar Moss which, one can only conjecture, might have been for peat extraction.

More gorse beautifies the railway cuttings and embankments in springtime. The line appears to provoke a boundary of sorts between fertile farmland to the north and those peaty mosslands to the south, long since afforested and, as such, lacking the dramatic sense of loneliness they must once have exuded. Sphagnum Balticum, a rare mossland plant, is native to Racks Moss, but has had its habitat threatened by indiscriminate conifer planting.

MOSSLANDS give way to suburbia as the railway reaches the periphery of Dumfries. On the wall of a bus garage, flaking paintwork recalls the heyday of a luxury coach service operated by Western SMT between Glasgow and London. The site of Dumfries Motive Power Depot (12G/68B/67E) has been taken over by the county constabulary; Black Marias where once there were Black Fives. Old photographs illustrate a handsome six road building, double-bayed with lofty gables and round-arched entrances surmounted by rising tiers of similarly round-topped windows. Opened in 1878, it was the work of Andrew Galloway, not P. G. Woodhouse's 'Braces King', but the Glasgow & South Western Railway's civil engineer of the same name who used essentially the same design at Hurlford (Map 10) and Ayr (Map 17). It is difficult to think of a more elegantly designed group of engine sheds anywhere else in the British Isles; they could equally well have functioned as large non-conformist chapels. Until the end windows were unsympathetically infilled by the LMS, it was possible for those of a railway bent to look down from St Mary's Street bridge and view the steamy monsters at rest within. Confound those who ordered its demolition, it would have made a wonderful sports hall, a better fate than the neighbouring goods shed, incorporated into a supermarket! Oh well, you sigh, the engine shed may have gone, but at least Dumfries has recently regained the status of a signing-on point for train crew.

Thirty-three miles out from Carlisle the train pulls into DUMFRIES station. On the run from both the English police and German spies, Richard Hannay woke here 'just in time to bundle out and get into the slow Galloway train'. *The Thirty-Nine Steps* has outlived the railway timetable, and now if you wish to follow in John Buchan's literary footsteps it's a bus which awaits you on the station forecourt. Dumfries also appeared in the guise of 'Gledmouth' in Buchan's novel *Castle Gay*.

The station's north-facing bays have been filled in, though the handsome cast iron canopies have been retained, and it is perhaps sadly a peculiarly British failing that the empty space beneath them has not been made to function more imaginatively, perhaps as a cafe with an indoor garden, or a gallery, two existing and worthwhile activities relegated to less characterful accommodation on the up platform.

And yet despite a failure to grasp such opportunities, Dumfries remains one of Scotland's more handsome stations, the salmon-coloured sandstone of its buildings arrayed gracefully upon a gentle curve. Staffed and well maintained, and home also to a

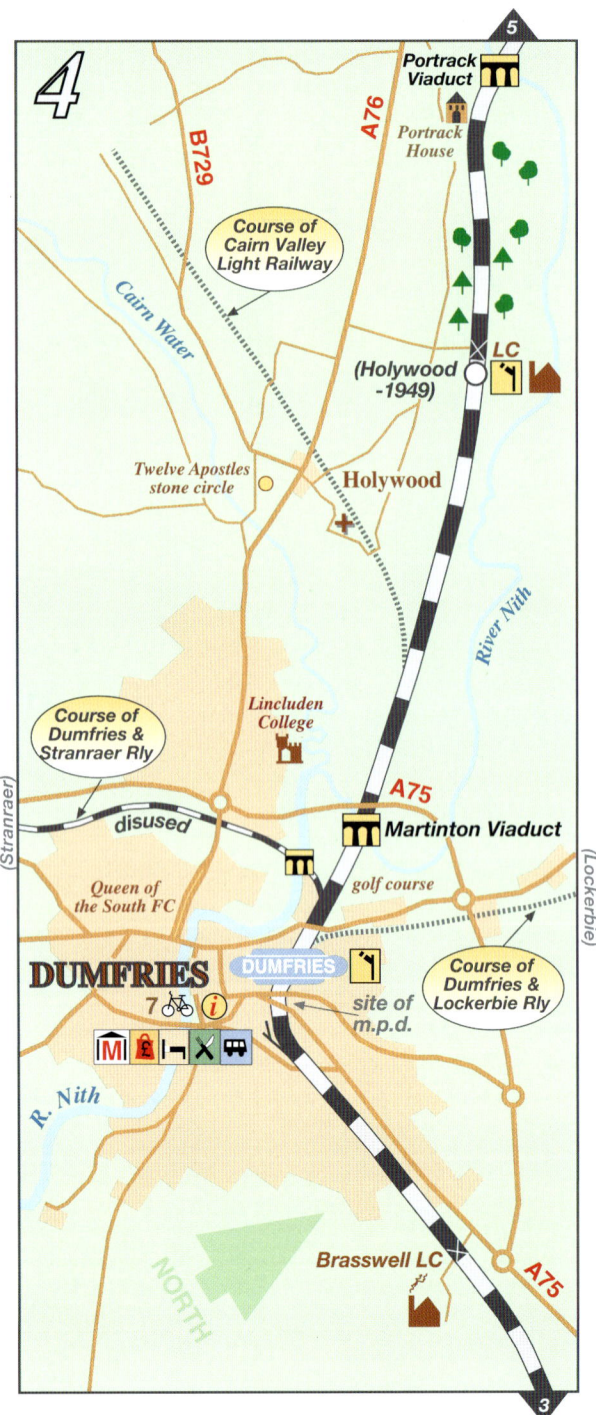

car hire company, it seems to share its confidence with the town on its doorstep. Further dignity is added to the scene by the presence of a handsome, cupola-topped Station Hotel, designed for the Glasgow & South Western by W. J. Milwain in 1896. One of four Sou' Western station hotels (three of which remain very much in use) it stayed in railway ownership until 1972.

Of the four railway lines which once radiated from Dumfries, solely the most senior of these, the Nith Valley route, remains. In order of divergence others led to Lockerbie, Stranraer (via Castle Douglas) and Moniaive. The Dumfries, Lochmaben & Lockerbie Railway was a subsidiary of the Caledonian Railway and opened in 1863. As far as the Caley were concerned it provided a strategic link between their main line and the Portpatrick & Wigtownshire Joint Railway in which they had an interest. From the Glasgow & South Western point of view it allowed their rival uncomfortable access to one of their strongholds. Indeed the line proved useful in channelling goods to and from south-west Scotland; notably an evening departure carrying Carnation condensed milk from Maxwelltown to Perth. There were also lucrative quarries at Locharbiggs, four miles east of Dumfries. Workmen's trains ran to and from the Arrol-Johnston motor works at Heath Hall, but for most of the line's existence the passenger service averaged just four trains per day in each direction. Passenger services ceased in 1952, goods still used the line for another fourteen years. On 15th May, 1965, *Flying Scotsman* was a notable visitor to the route, hauling an excursion returning to Lincoln over the by then weed-strewn track, because it was too long to fit the turntable at Dumfries.

If the line to Lockerbie never amounted to much more than a rural by-way, the same could never be said about the 'Port Road', the still much mourned direct railway between Dumfries and Stranraer. Today it is 135 miles by rail between the two towns, until 1965 it was a mere 73 miles. And even now, forty years after the line's closure on the recommendation of Doctor Beeching, its reinstatement remains an occasionally whispered pipe dream.

One may pragmatically measure the 'Port Road's' abandonment as an alternative to the traffic-weary A75, or more poetically regret its absence from the list of Scotland's most scenic railway routes. It is part of a sad roll-call of lines no longer capable of being travelled over; the Waverley route and Fife Coast line being fellow casualties which spring readily to mind. Those who poke such easy fun at railway enthusiasts might ruefully bear in mind that it is a pastime of necessity often endured within the bittersweet melancholy of the past tense. As if to taunt those who most regret its closure, a rusty line of track still twists away from the main line, though reaching only as far as Maxwelltown. There have been suggestions that this mothballed line might be revived for the use of oil trains from Grangemouth.

Skew-arched, Martinton Viaduct carries the line to Kilmarnock over the River Nith as the train makes its escape from Dumfries. It was designed in 1850 by John Miller whose more dramatic works will be encountered as the journey progresses. His son, incidentally, was responsible for the similarly low-slung viaduct carrying the Castle Douglas line over the Nith nine years later.

After passing beneath the ring-road it is possible to discern, on the western side of the line, the earthworks of the former branch line to Moniaive. Prettily known as the Cairn Valley Light Railway, this 17 mile by-way lived its brief forty-four year existence in obscurity, being a beneficiary of the Light Railways Act which enabled it to be built on a low budget and

opened for traffic in 1905. In its early years passenger services were in the hands of steam railcars, but latterly a single carriage and steam locomotive sufficed.

The level crossing at Holywood can, however, lay claim to being the last wheel-operated crossing in Scotland. Apparently the signaller makes use of an hourglass to fine judge the approach of southbound trains on their way down from Thornhill. The grounds of nearby Portrack House contain the formal Garden of Cosmic Speculation, developed by the American architectural critic Charles Jencks and his late wife, Maggie Keswick; benefactoress of the Maggie Centres. The ground are opened to the public to raise money for charity once a year through the Scottish Garden Scheme. The new award-winning Portrack Viaduct spans the Nith in propinquity, its huge red truss construction designed by Scott Wilson in association with Charles Jencks. There is an elegant simplicity about the structure, alongside which fragments of the previous bridge and items of rolling stock have been incorporated as part of the neighbouring gardens.

Portrack

Charles Jencks

Dumfries

Holywood

Coal train and conifers, Upper Nithsdale

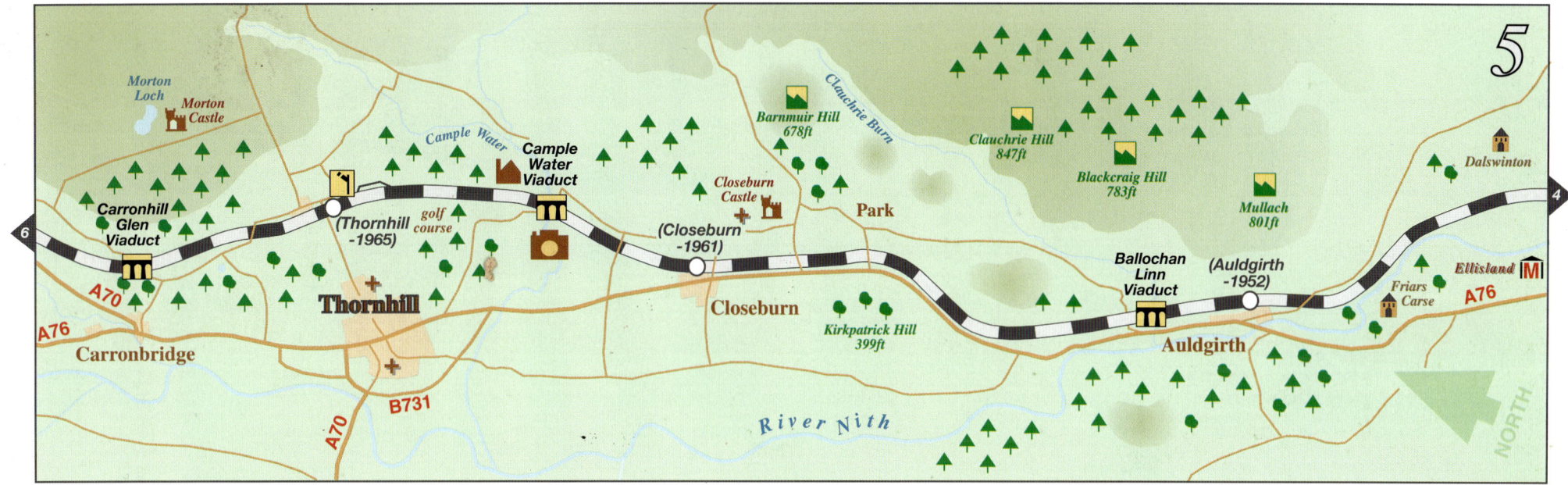

HIGHER ground begins to cuddle uxoriously closer to the railway as Nithsdale grows lovelier with each successive mile. It crosses your mind that great poetry could be inspired by such a landscape, which of course it has. A whitewashed farm can just be seen through trees on the far bank of the Nith. This is Ellisland where Robert Burns arrived in May, 1788 and farmed for three years. His landlord was Patrick Miller of Dalswinton, which can be seen from the right hand side of a train travelling north. Miller was a banker and man of many parts who had reputedly made and spent three fortunes. On a lochan within the policies of Dalswinton, a scaled-down prototype of one of the world's first steamboats was put through its paces, and it is possible that Burns was an onlooker.

Miller had offered Burns the choice of three farms to rent. Aparently it was the poet in him, attracted to the riverside setting, rather than the practical farmer, which led to Ellisland being selected, for it was palpably the least fertile of the trio. On this account, three difficult years ensued, though not because Burns was necessarily a bad farmer, indeed, he is credited with introducing Ayshire dairy cattle into Nithsdale. But despite the difficulty that he and Jean Armour encountered in working Ellisland, paradoxically he was at his most productive as a poet. Some of his greatest works were written here: *Tam O' Shanter*, *Sweet Afton*, *Auld Lang Syne* and *The Wounded Hare*, for example. In what spare time he could muster he would walk northwards along the riverbank to meet his boon companion Capt. Robert Riddell of Friars Carse. The estate had been the location of a monastic outpost of Melrose Abbey: Annie Laurie (of Scots song immortality) had died here in 1764. Riddell had erected a small, habitable folly in the grounds to which the poet repaired to write, fuelled more often than not, by liberal amounts of liquor.

To add to his meagre income, Burns began working as an Exciseman, but by 1791, Burns was despairing of ever making the farm pay its way. 'This farm has undone my enjoyment of myself' he wrote. He and Jean upped to Dumfries and Burns became a full-time 'gager', or Riding Officer, for the Excise, with ten parishes of Upper Nithsdale as his beat. For a while Burns continued to visit Friars Carse. But the friendship foundered after the poet had one evening drunkenly, and to his subsequent shame, re-enacted the *Rape of the Sabine Women* in mixed company.

Another trio of closed stations features in this stretch of the journey; a dozen of them, no less, since leaving Carlisle. AULDGIRTH faded by the wayside in 1952, yet the remains of the station are still visible amongst a rash of new housing. At CLOSEBURN - where the Glasgow Paisley Kilmarnock & Ayr Railway met the Glasgow Dumfries & Carlisle Railway in 1850, thereafter amalgamating to form the Glasgow & South Western - a coal merchant and a dealer in wooden pallets continue to occupy the goods yard. When the station was open it served a Victorian model village with a number of notable buildings. The handsome parish church dates from 1878 and seems far too substantial in its setting, and perhaps more English in style than one would expect. Over a thousand German POW's were housed in Nissen huts at Carronbridge during the Second World War.

An up loop, restored as recently as 2000 and controlled by a redbrick signal box of functional design, provides a useful facility for the recessing of coal trains, and heralds THORNHILL. This station's closure was one of the more irrational on the line. Dumfries & Galloway Council have been keen to have the station re-opened for a number of years. It serves an area with an adult population in the region of four thousand, the platforms remain in situ, and yet progress is seemingly stymied by the usual welter of bureaucracy, inflated costs and unnecessarily high specifications which attach themselves to such opportunities.

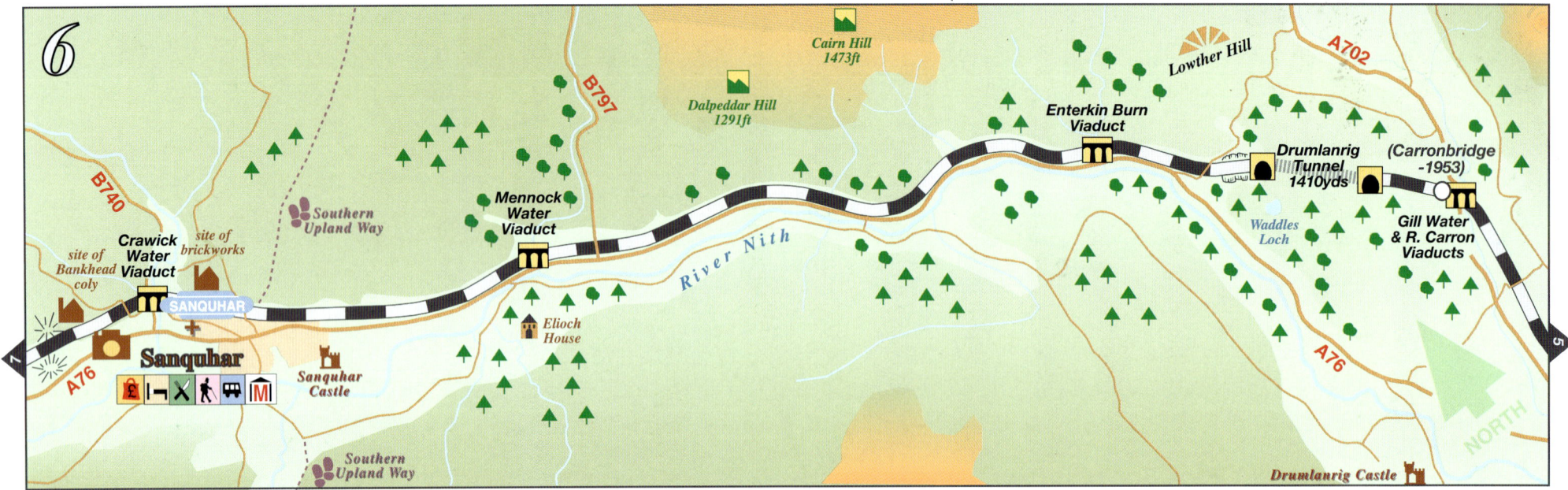

THE line climbs at 1 in 150 to the southern portal of Drumlanrig Tunnel. CARRONBRIDGE station lay a couple of country miles to the north of the handsome ducal village which lent it its name. An obelisk to the east of the line commemorates local soldiery killed in the First World War. The A702 passes beneath the railway and heads for the picturesque Dalveen Pass, overlooked by the prominent summit of Lowther Hill with its radar station like a giant golf ball perched invitingly on a tee. At 2378ft this is one of the prized 'Corbetts' of the Southern Uplands in fell-walking and mountaineering circles. Its neighbour, Green Lowther, also carries radar towers, but otherwise these hills remain alluringly bare-shouldered.

The train clatters cacophonically through Drumlanrig Tunnel which derives its title from the neighbouring castle, 17th century seat of the Dukes of Buccleuch. (4)6230, one of Sir William Stanier's famous Coronation Class steam locomotives was named *Duchess of Buccleuch*: it would have seen regular use on the line in its years as a Polmadie, Glasgow based engine. It is a shame that since 1953 you can no longer alight at Carronbridge and walk along traffic-free roads to the castle. Nowadays it is a popular visitor attraction accessible almost exclusively to those with a car at their disposal.

Beyond the tunnel the railway, running briefly downhill at 1 in 200, traverses a shelf above the Nith Gorge. In terms of scenic drama this marks the Nith Valley route's zenith. One might almost be somewhere along the Highland Main Line; though, as is increasingly the case on many of Scotland's scenic lines, burgeoning vegetation hampers full appreciation. Similarly, those who enjoy photographing trains in a landscape setting are thwarted by tree growth and denied the sort of views earlier generations of railway photographers took for granted. It is a paradox that in an era of increased mobility and more sophisticated photographic equipment, the window of opportunity has been firmly rendered opaque by the relaxation of lineside maintenance regimes. Nevertheless, with its red ballast, the railway remains perfectly assimilated into the landscape it passes through, which is more than can be said of the parallel A76, upon which the traffic rarely seems to abate.

The B-road to Wanlockhead - Scotland's 'highest village', and home of the Leadhills & Wanlockhead two foot gauge tourist railway, the loftiest adhesion worked railway in Britain - crosses the railway, wriggling eastwards into hills now gorgeously heather-clad but once extensively lead-mined.

Eliock House may be glimpsed through the trees to the west of the line. In rivalry with Cluny in Perthshire, it is the disputed birthplace of 'the Admirable Crichton'. Not J. M. Barrie's perfect butler, but James Crichton the 16th century polymath who graduated from St Andrews University at the ridiculously early age of fourteen and 'flashed like a meteor across the literary firmament of Europe' before tragically dying in a street brawl in Italy aged just twenty-two.

The ruins of Sanquhar Castle, viewed above caravans and a petrol station, lead to the town of SANQUHAR (pronounced 'sank-her') whose station was peremptorily abandoned in the Beeching era, only to be sensibly granted a new lease of life in 1994. 'Alight Here for the Southern Upland Way' urge the signs, and that is certainly an idea not without its temptations, even if this is the only railway station serving the 212 mile route between Portpatrick on the south-west coast and Cockburnspath on the eastern seaboard. Closer at hand, Sanquhar is not without its own aspects of interest, especially if you have an enthusiasm for industrial archaeology, for this was once a busy mining town whose Bankhead pit produced steam coal for the G&SWR, and whose brickworks supplied materials for the lining of many a railway tunnel.

Sanquhar Bings

New Cumnock cloudscape

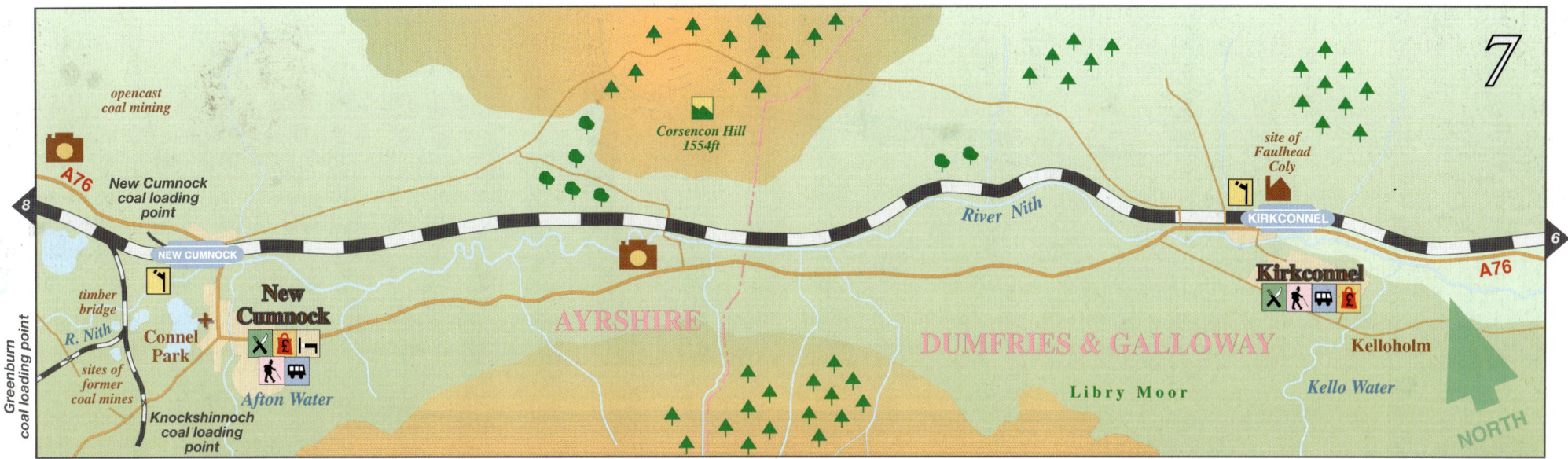

PICTURE yourself aboard the *Thames-Clyde Express*, the line's crack train of yore, Jubilee, Royal Scot, A3 or Peak-hauled and eating up the miles. The down train left London St Pancras at 10.15 am, reversed at Leeds and, travelling via the Settle & Carlisle and Nith Valley routes, reached Glasgow St Enoch nine and a half hours later - Britain, for the better one surmises, seemed a bigger place in those days.

How agreeably the landscape would be flashing past your window: agreeably, that is, until yet another coal mining region impinged itself upon Upper Nithsdale's pastorality; for at KIRKCONNEL the slate rooftop's of miner's terraces once more expunged the angler's beats. Fauldhead Colliery, as the local pit was called, had opened in Queen Victoria's Golden Jubilee year and, in common with Bankhead, had proved a significant source of steam coal for the Glasgow & South Western and its successors. Little wonder, then, that with steam having been withdrawn from South-west Scotland in 1966, the colliery's days were numbered, even with a respectable output in the region of a thousand tons per day.

Kirkconnel's most famous son is Alexander Anderson who was born here in 1845. He was employed by the G&SWR as a 'surfaceman', a pseudonym he adopted for his books of poetry. His wide interests belied his humble occupation, for it is safe to say that few of his contemporaries at work along the Nith Valley line were familiar with great works of poetry and philosophy whilst being capable of speaking French, German and Italian and reading Latin and Greek. One of his collections of verse was called *Songs of the Rail* and it includes poems with railway themes such as *Railway Dreamings*, *What the Engine Says* and *On the Engine by Night*. Anderson worked on the railway for seventeen years before being tempted away by academe and rising to the post of Chief Librarian at Edinburgh University. There is a memorial to him beside the parish church.

A brief interval of pure countryside intervenes as the railway runs beneath the flank of Corsencon Hill. The Nith corkscrews alongside the line, cascading down through shallow rock pools. The river has its source about five miles north-east of Dalmellington and journeys fifty miles to its outfall in the Solway Firth. At New Cumnock it is joined by its tributary the Afton Water: Burns's 'Sweet Afton' of course. Upstream of Kirkconnel the river is fished for sea trout, but for reasons of conservation, not for salmon, as these head-waters are the spawning grounds for the rest of the river system. Fish numbers have dwindled from a high in the 1960s when perhaps five or six thousand fish might be landed annually. Nowadays figures are counted in hundreds rather than thousands. Somewhat implausibly, *Mission Impossible*

- a thriller starring Tom Cruise - was 'filmed' on the line hereabouts. Filmed, in the sense of the passing scenery, for the train itself, a French TGV, was computer generated!

Britain's tallest sempahore signal heralds NEW CUM-NOCK, a busy loading point for opencast coal. One of the connecting lines spans the Nith on a rare timber bridge. Whereas coal is won above ground now, in the past it was deep mined. Six pits flourished locally at the time of nationalisation in 1947: Bank, Bridgend and Burnfoot; Coalburn, Seaforth and Knockshinnoch. A seventh, Afton, was abandoned immediately following its acquisition by the National Coal Board. In the 1930s it had been the scene of experiments in the extraction of oil from coal. Knockshinnoch gained notoriety in 1950 when liquid peat burst into the workings, killing thirteen miners and trapping over a hundred others. Although the mine's main shaft had been sunk to a depth of over seven hundred feet, coal was being extracted little more than forty feet below the peat when the roof caved in and miners ran for their lives before an onrush of liquid sludge. Those that survived found themselves trapped below ground and prevented from rescue by gas. Two anxious days elapsed before the men were released from their underground prison by dint of using breathing apparatus which none of them had hitherto been trained in the use of.

HAVING been journeying due west through Upper Niths-dale, you are now heading due north. A picturesque sequence of lochs (lochans more accurately) accompanies the line's ascent to the summit at Polquhap, 616 feet above sea level. From Polquhap (pronounced 'Polcap') the line descends more or less all the way to Kilmarnock. From both sides of the train the land rises to distant peaks, and in clear weather you can see Benquhat Hill (1427ft) in the west and Wardlaw Hill (1631ft) in the east.

A rocky cutting precedes Cumnock. An imposing viaduct straddles the south-western outskirts of the town, and if you concentrate closely you can see where the line it carried passes beneath yours. These are the remains of a railway which once linked Ayr with the iron-making and coal-mining town of Muirkirk, a Glasgow & South Western service in Pre-Grouping days which connected with the Caledonian Railway at Muirkirk for onward conveyance to Lanark. What a fascinating cross-country journey that must have been, a forty-six and a half mile slice of Lowland Scotland characterised at one moment by bare moorland, the next by gritty little industrial Klondyke communities. A cursary glance at station names in old timetables speaks volumes of the route's inherent austerity: Trabboch, Drongan, Skares, Glenbuck (where Bill Shankly first played football for The Cherrypickers), Inches, Ponfeigh. Passenger services ceased west of Muirkirk in 1951, freight survived another thirteen years. The big viaduct you can see has been reinvented as a public right of way, all thirteen arches providing a worthwhile means of making one's way from one housing scheme to another seventy-five feet above Glaisnock Water; as valiant a survivor as a Roman aqueduct.

The watercourses in this part of the world inspired other great railway structures. Just past the site of CUMNOCK station (another irrational closure considering that this is the largest town between Dumfries and Kilmarnock) the line dramatically bridges a chasm cut by Lugar Water. This viaduct is the work of John Miller (1805-1883) who forged a highly successful engineering partnership with Thomas Grainger. Miller is thought to have considered the Lugar Water Viaduct his greatest work. It is difficult now to fully ascertain the number of arches, so high grow the trees about its piers. Somebody should create a society for the prevention of tree growth beside viaducts, for an over abundance of vegetation

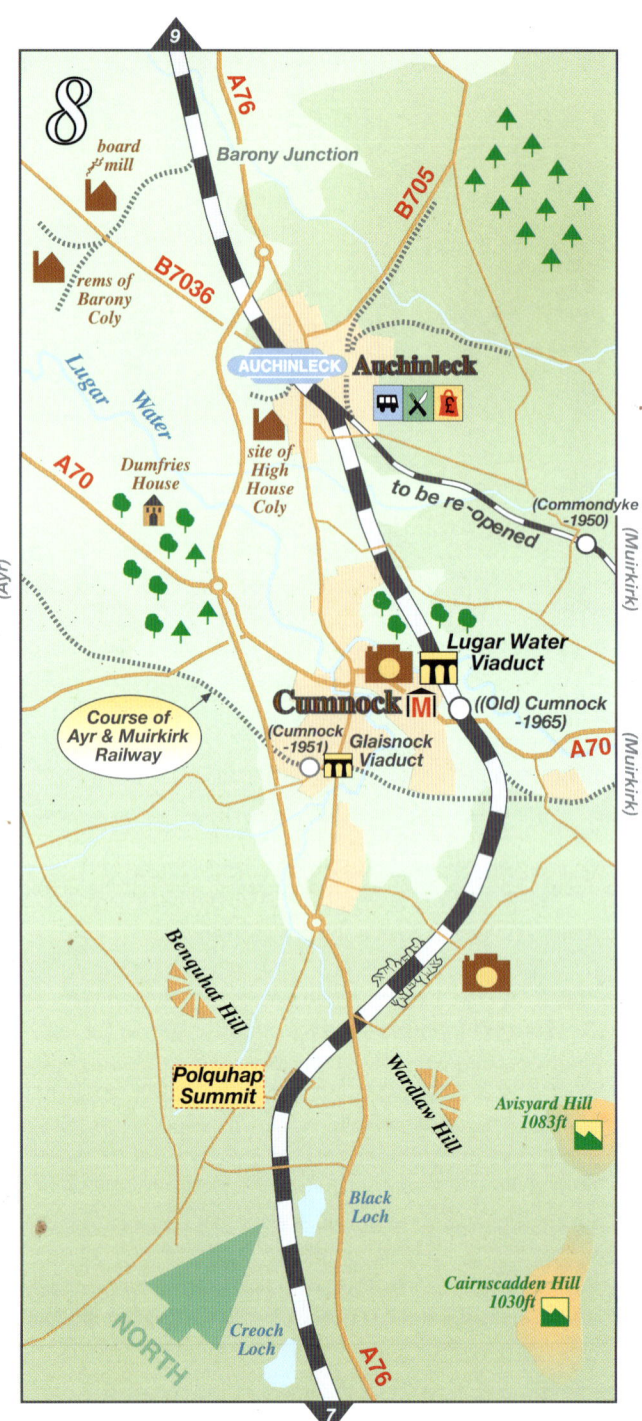

is tantamount to painting clothes on a Rubens nude. His fortune made, Miller retired early at the age of forty-five and pursued a career in politics, but his railway work is likely to stand the test of time as his real legacy.

Until recently, the viaduct afforded a birds-eye view of an open-air swimming pool, but this charming lido has inexplicably been demolished and grassed over as if it had never been. What Philistines: the pool was hand dug by miners; Keir Hardie's daughter performed the opening ceremony in 1936; it became the home of Cumnock & District Miners Amateur Swimming Club; in winter they covered it and used it for dancing; the first person to plunge into it the following Spring traditionally was awarded with a free season ticket for their foolhardiness.

Should you feel thwarted that Cumnock (with its Keir Hardie connections) cannot be visited by train, alight at AUCHINLECK and make your way back. Auchinleck also lost its passenger trains to Beeching, but they returned in 1984. Another (as yet incipient) comeback may concern revival of the branch which once led to Muirkirk via Cronberry as part of a scheme to create fresh access to opencast mines to the east of Cumnock. There were wayside halts at Commondyke and Lugar (once noted for its iron works and the birthplace in 1754 of William Murdoch inventor of gas lighting) and trains ran through to Muirkirk before withdrawal came in 1950.

During the train's brief pause at Auchinleck you snatch a view of sundry slate rooftops, a bus garage, a small football ground and an old colliery headstock; nothing, it is true, remotely prepossessing, but oozing atmosphere none the less. Disdainfully removed from all this (see Map 9) Auchinleck House was the childhood home of James Boswell who brought Dr Johnson to stay after their Tour of the Highlands in 1773. It is now available for holiday let under the auspices of the Landmark Trust. A mile to the south-west on the far bank of Lugar Water stands Dumfries House, a Palladian mansion designed by John and Robert Adam in 1759. It had its own remote station on the Ayr to Muirkirk line until 1949.

Pulling away from Auchinleck your gaze is drawn to a plume of white smoke to the west issuing from a board mill. Nearby stands another abandoned colliery headstock marking the site of Barony pit, the last NCB mine in Ayrshire when it closed in 1989.

Parklife, Lugar Water Viaduct

Sweet brig o' Ballochmyle

WHEN, in 1903, the Glasgow & South Western Railway eventually got round to building a three and a half mile branch to Catrine, it wasn't because they liked the sound of its pretty, girlish name, but because it had extensive cotton mills which they hoped they could cash in on. Considering that the mills were founded in 1787 by Claud Alexander of Ballochmyle and the altruistic David Dale (also involved with Arkwright and Owen at New Lanark) the branch came rather late in the day. And indeed its passenger services - usually operated by steam rail-motor colloquially known as the 'Catrine Caur' - lasted just forty years, being abandoned by the LMS during the Second World War; under the cloak of which they successfully camouflaged several railway and canal closures. David L. Smith wrote affectionately of 'The Caur' in *Tales of the Glasgow & South Western Railway*, describing 'her' as 'a game little thing and a grand steamer' which 'you could kindle in the morning at Ayr with a barrowful of coal' before operating the 6am workers' special to Annbank, and thence heading on to Mauchline to begin the day's shuttle service to and from Catrine. The first return trip would include the additional load of a bogie composite and milk van. In *The Lost Railway Lines of Ayrshire* (ISBN 1 872350 27 5) Alisdair Wham relates how burglars, over generous with their explosives, blew up the station building in 1909, rather than just the door of the safe as intended. Goods trains continued to ply the branch until 1964, the year following the destruction of the main cotton mill by fire. Little remains of the branch now, though its course can be briefly discerned by hawk-eyed passengers from passing trains at the site of Brackenhill Junction.

There is unfortunately, however, little opportunity to reflect on the history of the Catrine branch before encountering one of the main line's most spectacular engineering triumphs, Ballochmyle Viaduct. As with the Lugar Water Viaduct (Map 8) this is again the work of John Miller and, on account of its massive central span of 180 feet, the more feted. In its

red, locally quarried sandstone, it appears positively organic. From the train it is difficult to fully appreciate the towering triumph of the structure, nor are photographers much better served owing to the density of trees which grow on either side of the steeply banked River Ayr. A winter's day when the branches are bare is the best time to follow the footpath along the north bank of the river to fully savor Miller's masterpiece.

With the words of 'Fareweel sweet Ballochmyle' on their scholarly lips, Burns aficionados will be turning their thoughts to Mauchline where the poet lived for four years from 1784, a consideration which cut no ice with Beeching when he instigated the station's closure, scant trace of which remains. Thus it is sadly impossible to alight on the trail of Jean Armour (not to mention the other Belles of Mauchline), Johnnie Doo, and Poosie Nansie, but at least you can spare them a passing thought as the train clatters over Mauchline Junction under the watchful eye of another refurbished G&SWR mechanical signal box. This oversees comings and goings on what is now a token-worked freight only line to and from Ayr. When Stranraer lost its direct trains from Dumfries via the Port Line in 1965, through services such as the Euston sleeper were diverted this way for ten years. Thereafter the line via Annbank was demoted for solely freight use, and even that traffic went into hibernation in the mid-Eighties prior to a boost in the coal trade. It is a fine sight to see a Class 66 come climbing off the curve with a heavy train of loaded coal hoppers making for the main line.

Mossgiel resonates in Burnsian circles for this was the location of the farm that Robert and his brother Gilbert farmed. Again, it is pleasurable to contemplate the poetry which might have materialised if Burns could have hung around another sixty years or so to witness Mossgiel Tunnel being dug by the navvies of the Glasgow Dumfries & Carlisle Railway. The distinctive memorial tower to the east of the railway celebrates the poet.

Emerging from Mossgiel's rocky northern approach cutting, the clear scar of another abandoned trackbed can be seen to the east of the line. This led to Mauchline Colliery, sunk in 1925 and abandoned in 1966. In National Coal Board days eight hundred miners earned a living here. Where, one wonders rhetorically, do their children and grand-children find work now - in call centres perhaps?

⑨

⑩

The Coal Lines

Mauchline
Annbank
Catrine
Auchinleck
Killoch Cumnock
Falkland Yard
Ayr
Greenburn
Knockshinnoch
Maybole
Chalmerston
Dalmellington

(not all stations shown)

To Ayr

A719

Cessnock Water Viaduct

A76

B744

Cessnock Water

Mossgiel Tunnel 680yds

plaque

National Burns Memorial

site of Mauchline Coly

freight only

B743

Mauchline

Mauchline Junction

(Mauchline -1965)

site of Ballochmyle Quarry

Blackside Hills

B743

Kingencleugh

B705

River Ayr

Lugar Water

Ballochmyle Viaduct

Catrine

(Catrine -1943)

A76

Course of Catrine Branch

NORTH

Brackenhill Junction

Auchinleck House

⑧

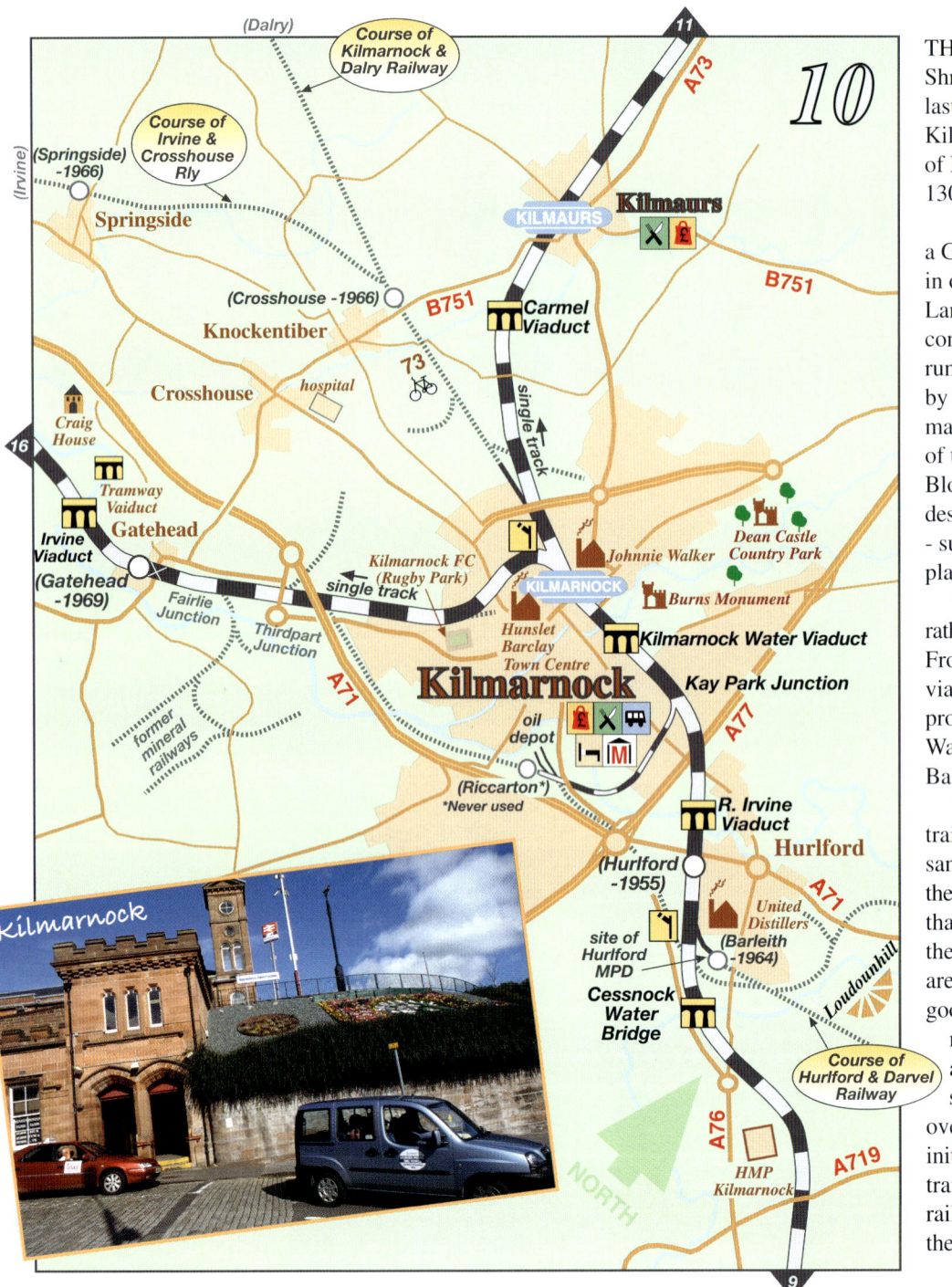

Map labels:

(Dalry)

Course of Kilmarnock & Dalry Railway

Course of Irvine & Crosshouse Rly

10

A73

(Irvine)

(Springside) -1966)

Springside

Kilmaurs

KILMAURS

(Crosshouse -1966)

B751

Knockentiber

B751

hospital

73

Crosshouse

Carmel Viaduct

16

Craig House

single track

Tramway Viaduct

Irvine Viaduct

Gatehead

(Gatehead -1969)

Fairlie Junction

Thirdpart Junction

single track

Kilmarnock FC (Rugby Park)

Dean Castle Country Park

Johnnie Walker

KILMARNOCK

Burns Monument

Hunslet Barclay Town Centre

Kilmarnock Water Viaduct

A71

Kilmarnock

Kay Park Junction

former mineral railways

oil depot

A77

(Riccarton*) *Never used

R. Irvine Viaduct

Hurlford

(Hurlford -1955)

A71

United Distillers

site of Hurlford MPD

(Barleith -1964)

Loudounhill

Cessnock Water Bridge

Course of Hurlford & Darvel Railway

NORTH

A76

HMP Kilmarnock

A719

11

9

Kilmarnock

THE line descends at 1 in 100 towards Kilmarnock. A. E. Housman wrote a poem about Shrewsbury Gaol in which the prisoners to be hung in the morning cannot sleep through their last night for the noise of the trains. Happily no such disturbances face the inmates of HMP Kilmarnock, but will it ever inspire great poetry? To the east look out for the volcanic outcrop of Loudon Hill (1035ft) where Robert the Bruce scored a notable victory over the English in 1307.

Bridging Cessnock Water for the second time, the railway reaches HURLFORD whence a Glasgow & South Western branch ran to the lace-making town of Darvel. Beyond Darvel, in one of its uneasy collaborations with 'The Caley', an extension was built to Strathaven in Lanarkshire, but traffic proved sparse and passenger services were withdrawn by 1939. Trains continued, however, to operate between Darvel and Kilmarnock until 1964, a number of them running through to Glasgow St Enoch. For many years such trains would regularly be hauled by 4-4-0 2P steam locomotives affectionately known to their crews as 'the wee black yins', many of which were allocated to Hurlford motive power depot, which stood at the bifurcation of the Darvel line. Here, also, was a community of railway workers housing known as 'The Blocks', whilst multitudinous sidings were provided for mineral trains, marshalled before despatch to Troon Harbour. Hurlford shed closed in 1966 and barely any trace of all this activity - supplemented by coal pits and the furnaces of the vast Portland Iron Works - remains, its place taken, rather blandly it has to be said, by United Distillers whisky depot.

Crossing the River Irvine and the A77 trunk road (which connects Glasgow with Stranraer rather less romantically than the railway) the train encounters the suburban fringes of Kilmarnock. From Kay Park Junction a line originally laid to allow trains to run from Glasgow to Troon via Kilmarnock without reversal - but never regularly used for this purpose - continues to provide access to an oil terminal. A twenty-three arch viaduct carries you over Kilmarnock Water and offers a glimpse, to the north, of the elaborate Burns Monument, built out of Ballochmyle sandstone in 1879.

Various imposing towers, ecumenically and architecturally diverse, catch your eye as the train rumbles into KILMARNOCK station. This is a deceptively imposing affair, essayed in sandstone the colour of Tandoori trout, and dominated by an Italianate tower. Entrance from the lower street level is effected via a crenellated gateway which lends the misleading impression that you are entering a Tudoresque seat of learning. An ornamental garden clock strengthens the station's picturesque appeal, and furthermore, a good proportion of the elevated platforms are covered by glazed canopies supported by cast iron brackets bearing G&SWR initials. All good and well until you delve deeper and expose many empty rooms, no refreshment facilities, no toilets, and even visual display screens which seldom appear to function. They might as well resort to fingerposts, the brackets of which can still be discerned on a number of supporting columns. Instead, one is directed to departing trains by disembodied injunctions over a crackling tannoy. Flaking plaques recall the ephemeral enthusiasms of moribund initiatives; long-forgotten photo-opportunities for Provosts and Councillors. And yet changing trains at 'Killie' has its compensations, especially if you are attuned to the latent dignity of railway installations. Close your eyes and conjure up the image of 'The Pullman' leaving for the south, a term in currency years after the last Midland Railway Pullman Car worked through to St Pancras; connecting services rejoicing under the terminology of 'Pullman Pups'.

Two of Kilmarnock's most prestigious firms have premises overlooking the west end of the railway station: the whisky blenders Johnnie Walker and the railway engineers Hunslet Barclay. Thus the names of two Ayrshire entrepreneurs live on in businesses which have survived two centuries of change. Johnnie Walker's famous red, black, gold and blue label whiskies may nowadays belong to a worldwide corporate concern whose other brands include Guinness, Smirnoff and Baileys, but the Kilmarnock connection remains strong. Born in 1805 of farming stock, John Walker had acquired his own grocery business by the age of fifteen and adapted techniques used in tea-blending to whisky. Subsequent generations of his family built on this expertise, and the global market consumes well over a hundred million bottles of whisky bearing the famous 'Striding Man' logo annually. The bottling plant beside the railway dates from as recently as the 1950s, but down in the town centre massive whisky bonds hark back to a previous, more elegant age.

Andrew Barclay may not be as much of a household name as Johnnie Walker, but he remains revered in railway circles. He was born nine years after Walker and although his life in business did not run as smoothly and upwardly - he was bankrupted on five occasions - his legacy is no less profound. From the first locomotive, built for the local Portland Iron Company of Hurlford in 1859, to the last, exported to an Indonesian company deriving oil out of palm trees in 1962, locomotives bearing the Barclay worksplate have provided sterling service all over the world. The vast majority were provided for industrial concerns, but in 1926 twenty-five Class 4F 0-6-0 locomotives were built under contract to the London Midland & Scottish Railway, a transaction not repeated owing to the fact that Barclays lost money on the contract! Amongst many Scottish customers was the Campbeltown & Macrihanish Light Railway of Argyll for whom two delightful narrow gauge 0-6-2 tank engines were supplied in 1907.

Barclay built up a reputation for reliable diesel shunting locomotives as well, British Railways, the National Coal Board, Central Electricity Generating Board, British Steel Corporation and the Ministry of Defence being amongst the recipients of such designs. In 1962 the Kilmarnock concern rather cheekily acquired the goodwill of the defunct North British Locomotive Company of Glasgow, a daring bid which has been likened to Ealing Studios tendering successfully for the goodwill of MGM. Ten years later Barclay merged with Hunslet, another famous locomotive engineering firm based in Leeds. In 1985 a fleet of Class 143 'Pacer' diesel units was produced for British Rail in association with the coachbuilders Alexander of Falkirk. These units originally worked in the North-east of England but now are based exclusively in South Wales. In 1990 the Class 20 diesel locomotives purchased by Hunslet-Barclay to haul its specialised weed-killing trains were charmingly named after female members of the firm's office staff. More recently Hunslet-Barclay have won contracts to refurbish First ScotRail Class 318 and 322 electric multiple units and it is good to see, as your train pulls out of the station, the Barclay name, still emblazoned on the rooftop of former offices recently converted into flats. A modern signal box oversees the junction of the Glasgow and Troon lines, both of which become single track. There is no longer any traffic into or out of the whisky bottling plant, whilst wagons stabled in former engineering sidings appear to have been there so long that they are imprisoned by vege-

tation. The Glasgow & South Western Railway works stood hereabouts, birthplace of many of the locomotive designs which sadly met an early demise upon the company's absorption into the London Midland & Scottish Railway in 1923. There were collieries and fireclay works in the neighbourhood as well, together with a line which ran in a north-westerly direction to Crosshouse before dividing further into routes to Irvine and Dalry. Dating from the early 1840s, the route to Dalry was the original means of travelling by rail between Kilmarnock and Glasgow.

Shaking free of Kilmarnock's outskirts, the train bridges Carmel Water and calls at KILMAURS, a wayside halt (closed in 1966 but re-opened in 1984) with an oddly constructed shelter which looks like something Faller or Vollmer might have provided for railway modellers of a German bent. Elevated above modestly rolling pastureland, in which ubiquitous Friesian milking herds appear to have ousted Ayrshire's own lovely breed, the railway offers panoramic views in a westerly direction, and if not hidden by rain squalls or mist, Arran's jagged outline predominates. Through cuttings lush with waving grasses, the gradient steepens to 1 in 87. Even lightweight diesel units seem to have their work cut out to complete the climb, goodness knows how footplate crews coped with the heavier and lengthier trains of the past. An atmosphere of lost grandeur hangs inevitably over this former main line, opened under the uncomfortably joint auspices of the Glasgow & South Western and Caledonian companies as the Glasgow Barrhead & Kilmarnock Railway in 1873.

Trains for Ayr, Girvan and Stranraer travel from Kilmarnock on a route which shadows the course of the Kilmarnock & Troon Rail Way of 1812, a four foot gauge plateway built to carry the Duke of Portland's coals from mines in the Kilmarnock area down to the docks at Troon for export to Ireland. Given the precise date of its opening, one might impishly describe it as an early 'overture' in railway construction, though there is no record of cannonfire accompanying the opening celebrations. Its simple coal wagons were horsedrawn, though before long it was attracting passengers as well, early day-trippers summoned to the growing reputation of Troon as a seaside resort.

Gathering speeds at which the plateway operators would have blanched, your train passes Rugby Park, the slightly disconcertingly titled home of Kilmarnock Football Club. 'Killie's' greatest moment came on the 24th April 1965 at Easter Road, Edinburgh when, away to their closest rivals Hearts, they won two-nil to clinch their first, and so far only, league title. More or less where the A71 dual-carriageway crosses the line stood Thirdpart Junction, the western end of the Kilmarnock avoiding line. Another line went off to the north-east, emphasising the sheer complexity of Kilmarnock's railway network at its zenith. And within half a mile stood Fairlie Junction entrance point to a network of colliery lines. At Gatehead you come upon the comparatively rare phenomenon, in latter-day Ayrshire at least, of a level crossing.

Irvine Viaduct carries the line across the eponymous river. Downstream stands Laigh Milton Viaduct, its senior partner, for this was where the original plateway crossed the river. One of the last works of the canal genius William Jessop, in recent years it has been handsomely restored and carries a public footpath. An imposing cream-washed mansion, Craig House, overlooks this historic structure, presumably glad that Fairlie No.3 Pit lies no longer on its doorstep. *Turn to Map 16 for continuation of this route description.*

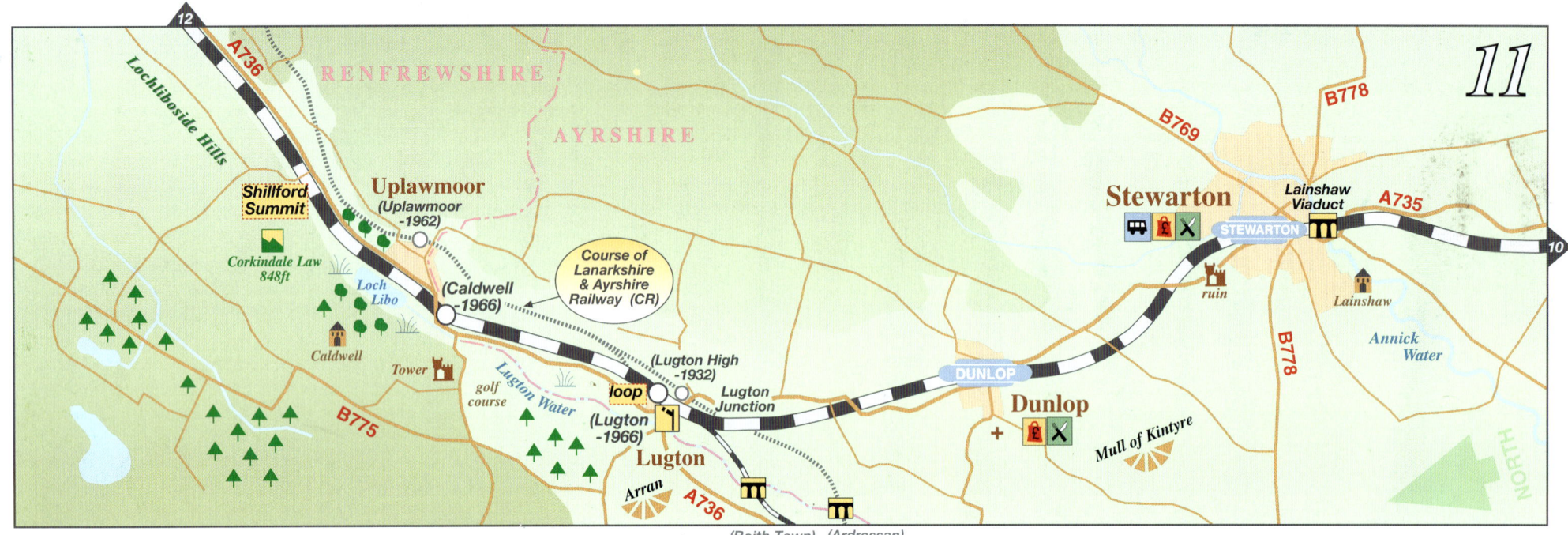

STEWARTON for bonnets, Dunlop for cheese - each wayside station sporting an indigenous industry on its doorstep: how their goods yards must have heaved and strained to cope with the business on offer. The ten arches of Lainshaw (aka Stewarton) Viaduct carry the line loftily over Annick Water; a tributary of the Irvine which manages to flow independently to within all but a mile or two of the Firth of Clyde. You catch a glimpse of paired Gothic gatehouses guarding the drive to Lainshaw House. One of its early 19th Century lairds spent his life in anticipation of the Second Coming and on occasions would assemble his household on the roof so as to be in a sufficient state of grace. In an earlier guise, Lainshaw had been the home of Margaret Montgomerie, a cousin of James Boswell. Having resolved never to marry, he made exception, being impressed with her 'particular merit', and trusting that she in turn would 'waive his faults'. For many years a sizeable corn mill stood on the riverbank alongside the viaduct.

Eighteen and a quarter miles short of Gorbals Junction, Stewarton doesn't look at its best from the station, reduced to a bare bus-sheltered platform since the line was singled, but parcels of smart new housing hint at a welcome and sensible increase in commuting. On 6th November 1974, shortly after

the former up line was lifted, the 07.15 Glasgow to Euston train, hauled by a Class 50 locomotive, became derailed at a set of redundant points. Fortunately, only one passenger received minor injuries, but perhaps more significantly there were only twenty-two of them occupying an enormous thirteen coach train!

Dunlop and Stewarton were closed in 1966, but re-opened less than a year later for a solitary train in each direction; having to wait until 1984 for the enhanced hourly service currently on offer. Money is now being spent on clearing the Sou' West main line as a diversionary route for Virgin Pendolinos, whilst the locally more significant redoubling of the section between Dunlop and Stewarton to provide a half-hourly frequency lies on hold, awaiting funding.

The gradient steepens to 1 in 75 and, emerging from a cutting, you encounter the slight ruin which is all that is left of Ravenscraig Castle. Before reaching Dunlop the views open out once more, and even the Mull of Kintyre can be traced on a clear day. A number of disused quarries in the vicinity once had rail links. DUNLOP station mirrors Stewarton in its state of far from titillating undress, but here at least the stone-built goods shed has survived the passage

of time.

Before Lugton is reached it is worth looking out from the left hand side of the train at what remains of the Lanarkshire & Ayrshire Railway. Two well-preserved overbridges come into view, followed by a magnificent eleven arch viaduct spanning Lugton Water. It all looks so pristine you half expect to witness a Caledonian boat train from Ardrossan Montgomerie Pier come sweeping round the curve to cross your line. But when you reach the site of the skew bridge which carried the L&A over the GB&K, all that is left is a melancholy pair of redbrick abutments.

The L&A is a perfect illustration of the ridiculous rivalry between the Caledonian and Glasgow & South Western companies. The Caledonian already enjoyed joint ownership of the Glasgow Barrhead & Kilmarnock line, but they resented sharing revenues with the Sou' Western. They found this state of affairs particularly galling with regard to the lucrative coal traffic between Lanarkshire and Ardrossan, and so a parallel route was opened in 1903. Within a few years, however, a new dock at Clydebank was siphoning off much of this trade. The Caley still found it convenient (or face-saving!) to route boat trains connecting with steamer services to Arran and the

Isle of Man along the L&A, but following the Grouping of the railways in 1923, when both of the bickering rivals were absorbed into the LMS, the line was run down and its local stations closed, though Uplawmoor survived as an unlikely suburban railhead until electrification was extended out as far as Neilston (Map 12) in 1962.

From LUGTON JUNCTION a branch led to Beith (Town) a once prosperous 'wee toon' in the Garnock Valley with a tobacco factory, textile mills and a brewery. Passenger services survived until 1962, in their heyday running through to St Enoch, but as traffic diminished becoming a simple shuttle service to and from Lugton operated by four-wheel railbuses. Until recently the line remained intact as far as Giffen to serve an armaments depot, though judging by the rust on the track and the weeds between the sleepers, it has become a victim of what we have almost forgotten to call the peace dividend. Nowadays Lugton's signal box sports double-glazing, an internal loo and cooking facilities, refinements previous incumbents of the box would presumably have waived their wages for. Usually, the passing of oncoming trains on this tokenless block section goes as smoothly as a synchronised dance routine, but if one or other of the trains is out of schedule you can find yourself contemplating over long the debatable charms of Lugton Moss.

Underway once again, the train passes the remnants of Caldwell station, which once doubled as 'Tannochbrae' for the purposes of filming the original black & white Dr Finlay series, televised in the nineteen-sixties. Caldwell traditionally marked the crossing of the county boundary between Ayrshire and Renfrewshire, though nowadays this has been bureaucratically refined into *North* Ayrshire and *East* Renfrewshire. Loch Libo briefly introduces a quasi 'highland' feel to proceedings - Oban or Kyle of Lochalsh might plausibly be the next stop. A steepish climb then leads to Shillford and the summit of the line, some five hundred feet above sea level. 'Nine meenits f'ae The Shillford tae The Gorbals' is how the old Sou' Western drivers reckoned their schedule, something your Class 156 diesel unit will be hard pressed to achieve!

Swan Lake - Loch Libo

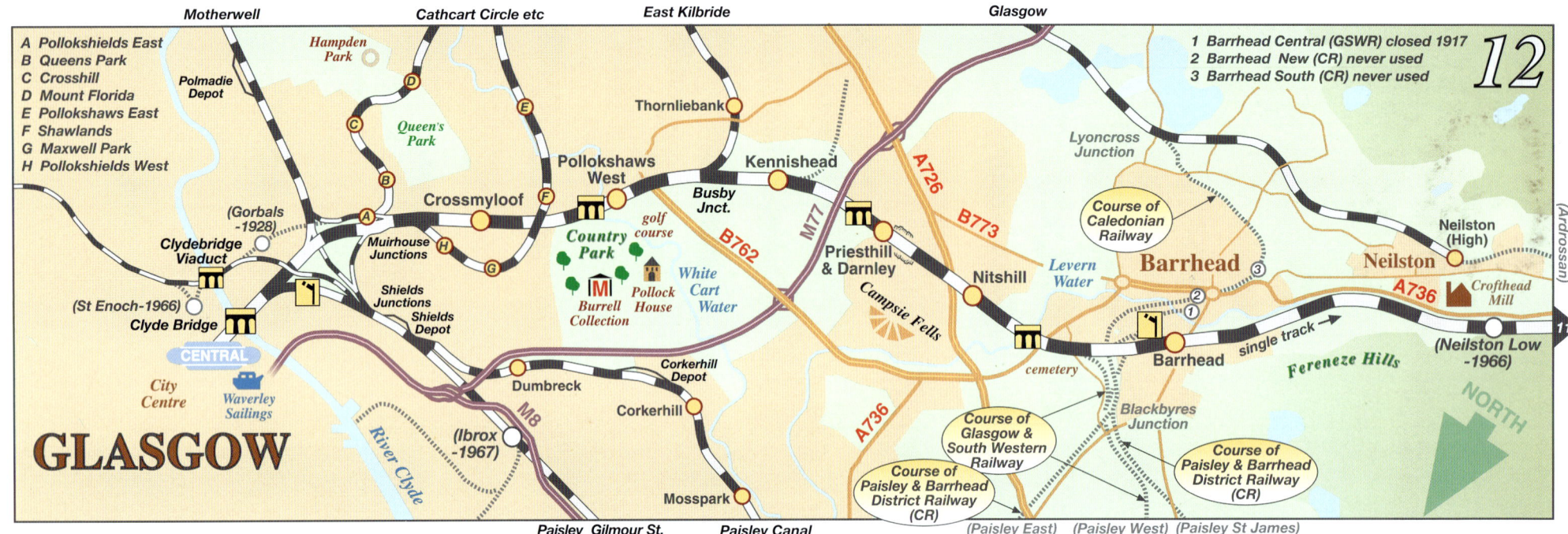

A Pollokshields East
B Queens Park
C Crosshill
D Mount Florida
E Pollokshaws East
F Shawlands
G Maxwell Park
H Pollokshields West

1 Barrhead Central (GSWR) closed 1917
2 Barrhead New (CR) never used
3 Barrhead South (CR) never used

12

Hampden Park

Polmadie Depot

Queen's Park

Thornliebank

Lyoncross Junction

Course of Caledonian Railway

Pollokshaws West   Kennishead   Neilston (High)

Crossmyloof   Busby Jnct.   A726   B773   Barrhead   Neilston

(Gorbals -1928)

Clydebridge Viaduct   Muirhouse Junctions   golf course   Country Park   M   Burrell Collection   Pollock House   White Cart Water   B762   Priesthill & Darnley   Campsie Fells   Nitshill   Levern Water   A736   Crofthead Mill

(St Enoch-1966)   Shields Junctions   Shields Depot

Clyde Bridge

CENTRAL

City Centre   Waverley Sailings   Corkerhill Depot   Barrhead   single track   Ferenze Hills   (Neilston Low -1966)   11

cemetery

GLASGOW   (Ibrox -1967)   M8   Dumbreck   Corkerhill   Blackbyres Junction   NORTH

Course of Glasgow & South Western Railway

Course of Paisley & Barrhead District Railway (CR)

Mosspark   Course of Paisley & Barrhead District Railway (CR)

River Clyde

Paisley Gilmour St.   Paisley Canal   (Paisley East)   (Paisley West)   (Paisley St James)

(Ardrossan)

BUCKETING downhill at 1 in 69, past dank retaining walls, which successfully obscure the outriding town of Neilston, the train encounters Crofthead, a gargantuan textile mill, disused since the early nineteen-nineties and crying out for imaginative refurbishment. Perhaps its setting beneath wuthering volcanic braes is against it; perhaps it needs a Jonathan Silver, as did Saltaire in *Iron Roads North of Leeds.*

Beneath the Ferenze Hills the train spins on, swishing down on welded track, branches brushing the windows until the countryside gives up the unequal struggle and surrenders to Glasgow's outer suburbs. Suddenly the brakes go on for BARRHEAD, and if you've been flummoxed by the density of rival railway networks in Ayrshire hitherto, Renfrewshire's will have you reeling. It is extraordinary that a small town such as Barrhead boasted four stations, and even more mystifying when you consider that two of them were built but never used. Once again, intensive rivalry between the Glasgow & South West and the Caledonian lay behind so elaborate an over provision, though ironically on this occasion they were both beaten - by Glasgow's and Paisley's burgeoning network of electric tramways.

In the bay platform - adjacent to a sizeable goods shed -

a stopping train may impatiently be waiting to follow in your non-stop footsteps. Beyond the opposite through platform lies the quaint little Dunterlie Park ground of Arthurlie Football Club, where they are still basking in the afterglow of dumping mighty Celtic out of the cup - in 1896!

Picking up speed on the final lap, your train skirts a huge cemetery overlooking the Levern Water, a tributary of the White Cart which itself flows out into the widening Clyde at Renfrew. By Nitshill the gradient bottoms out and suburban stations grow more frequent. Busby Junction marks the egress of the East Kilbride branch. From Pollokshaws West you can easily reach Pollok House and the home of the fabulous Burrell Collection. Sir William Burrell was a wealthy shipping magnate who bequested an enormous collection of antiquities and works of art to the City of Glasgow. A Class 47 diesel locomotive was named in his honour in 1983. Pollokshaws viaduct carries the line across White Cart Water.

At Crossmyloof a Morrisons supermarket charmlessly occupies the site of a vanished ice rink which in happier days formed an integral part in the social life of many a Glaswegian - though perhaps the same might sadly be said of the supermarket now.

Into a land of red and pink sandstone tenements runs the train. From Muirhouse Junctions, beneath electric wires, the Cathcart Circle sets off on its rotary peregrination of some of south Glasgow's most valuable real estate, less a railway, it has been said down the generations, than a means of meeting and subsequently marrying the opposite sex.

Traditionally, trains from Carlisle, Kilmarnock and Barrhead would have crossed the Clyde into Glasgow St Enoch, the Glasgow & South Western Railway's majestic terminus with its paired, arched train sheds and six storey hotel. It was arguably the most characterful of the city's four termini, but architecture and atmosphere were not prime considerations when British Rail decided to concentrate south Clydeside railway operations on Glasgow Central in 1966.

And so the Caledonian Railway had the last laugh. Terminating trains vault the Clyde in a manner reminiscent of crossing the Thames into Charing Cross - happily you are not greeted by a Glasgow Kiss. An impish sign on the Clyde Bridge reminds you that Carlisle is just 102 miles away, but you know better, and in journeying via Dumfries have confirmed that the real essence of travel has no direct correlation with time and distance.

Glasgow Paisley Ayr
STRANRAER LARGS

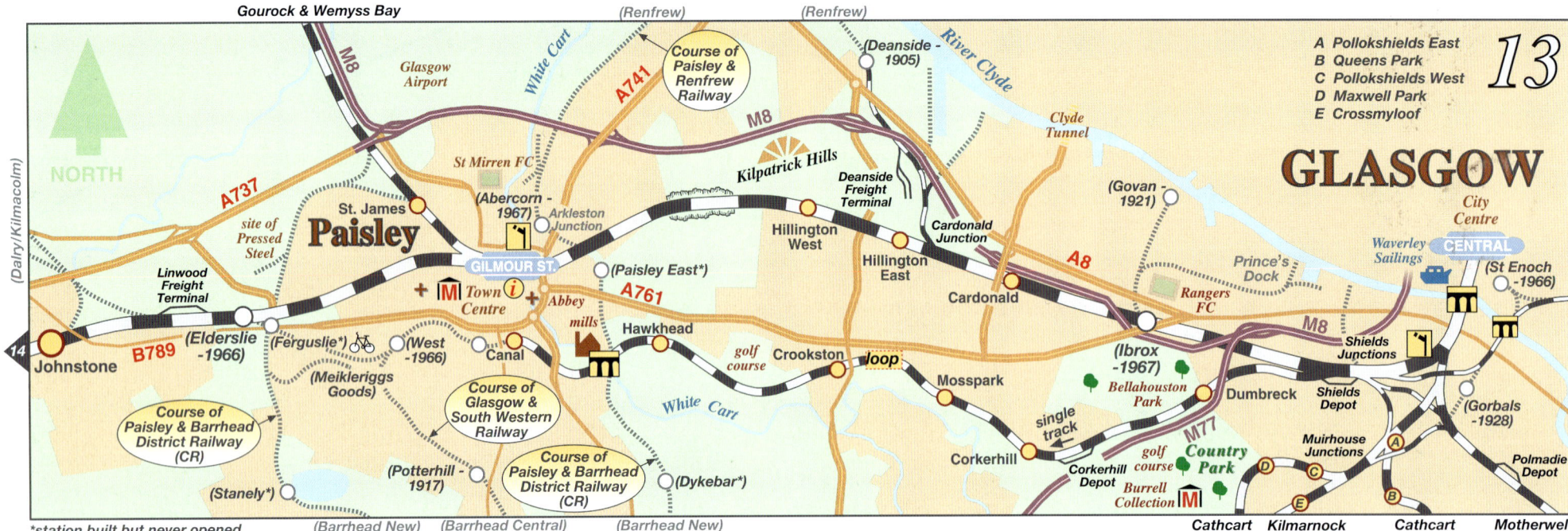

(map labels)

(Renfrew) (Renfrew)

Course of
Paisley &
Renfrew
Railway

(Deanside -
1905)

River Clyde

M8

A741

M8

Glasgow
Airport

White Cart

Clyde
Tunnel

13

A Pollokshields East
B Queens Park
C Pollokshields West
D Maxwell Park
E Crossmyloof

NORTH

A737

site of
Pressed
Steel

St Mirren FC

(Abercorn -
1967)

Arkleston
Junction

St. James

Paisley

Kilpatrick Hills

Deanside
Freight
Terminal

Deanside
Freight
Terminal

Hillington
West

Cardonald
Junction

(Govan -
1921)

A8

GLASGOW

City
Centre

Waverley
Sailings

CENTRAL

GILMOUR ST.

Town
Centre

Abbey
mills

(Paisley East*)

A761

Hillington
East

Cardonald

Prince's
Dock

Rangers
FC

M8

(St Enoch
-1966)

14 Johnstone

B789

(Elderslie
-1966)

Linwood
Freight
Terminal

(Ferguslie*)

(Meikleriggs
Goods)

(West
-1966)

Canal

Hawkhead

golf
course

Crookston

loop

Mosspark

single
track

Corkerhill

Ibrox
-1967)

Bellahouston
Park

Dumbreck

Shields
Junctions

Shields
Depot

Muirhouse
Junctions

(Gorbals
-1928)

Polmadie
Depot

Course of
Glasgow &
South Western
Railway

Course of
Paisley & Barrhead
District Railway
(CR)

White Cart

(Potterhill -
1917)

Course of
Paisley & Barrhead
District Railway
(CR)

(Dykebar*)

(Stanely*)

Corkerhill
Depot

golf
course

Country
Park

Burrell
Collection

*station built but never opened

(Barrhead New) (Barrhead Central) (Barrhead New)

Cathcart Kilmarnock Cathcart Motherwell

IF you were in a hurry to get from Glasgow to Paisley in the early part of the 19th Century, you caught the horse-drawn packet boat which plied the Glasgow Paisley & Johnstone Canal and the seven-mile journey took seventy-one minutes. Nowadays there are eight electric trains every hour, and sixty minutes have been shaved from the schedule; but would you be entirely human if you didn't wonder whether Progress is quite the guy he's got up to be? Not that the packet boat was always as idyllic as it sounds; four days after the opening ceremony in 1810, eighty-four people were drowned when the *Countess of Eglinton* overturned in Paisley Basin.

The canal, which never reached its goal of Ardrossan, became a victim of the Railway Age. The Glasgow & Paisley Joint line opened in 1840, and there was no looking back, however wistfully. In a heyday shared between the Caledonian and Glasgow & South Western railways, the G&PJ was the longest stretch of quadruple track in Scotland; very necessarily so, given that it needed capacity to cope with a kaleidoscope of fast and stopping passenger services to Renfrew, Gourock, Wemyss Bay, Ardrossan, Largs, Ayr and beyond, plus all manner of goods trains as well. But by the time the line to Gourock was electrified in 1967, double track was deemed

sufficient; though now there are plans for reinstatement of a third track as part of the scheme for a rail link to Glasgow Airport.

Once it would have been to St Enoch that you repaired to catch a train for Ayr, Stranraer or even Largs. But dear old St Enoch - Glasgow's most Gothic, soot-laden and thereby atmospheric terminus - has been demolished and replaced by a gargantuan shopping mall and ice rink: would Paris have been so profligate with its termini, or is the renunciation of valuable railway structures a peculiarly British trait?

Faute de mieux, Central exudes its own character - purpose and dignity in equal measure - and was voted Britain's 'Best Station' in 2005. Moreover the attractive SPT red and cream livery which adorns the majority of trains is a charming throwback to British Railways' 'blood & custard' colours. So it would be gratuitously churlish of you to look down your nose at the two-car diesel unit which presents itself for the hundred mile foray to the shores of Loch Ryan, wishing instead for a BRC&W Type 2, Swindon-built Inter-City unit, Clan Pacific, Stanier Black Five, or something from much, much deeper into the smoky past by Whitelegg, Manson, or Smellie? If plagued by such thoughts, draw consolation from

a Cranston's Angus Beef pie and a red Rioja from Marks & Spencer's food hall on Central station; display this guide conspicuously within the orbit of your travelling companions; and settle down to savour the journey as the diesel creeps cautiously out over the Clyde*.

Shields busy traction depot lies alongside the egress of the route to Paisley Canal, an off-beat and alternative way of reaching Renfrewshire's main town. It twists and turns curiously in comparison to the long straight stretches of the Glasgow & Paisley Joint, and the explanation for this lies in that it was built largely upon the bed of the Glasgow Paisley & Johnstone Canal by the G&SWR in 1885. Originally it rejoined the main line west of Paisley at Elderslie - thereby very usefully affording access to both the routes to Greenock and Kilwinning. Despite a vociferous campaign against closure, passenger services (which latterly had run out as far as Kilmacolm) were abandoned entirely in 1983, only to be reinstated in 1990. And whilst this guide's main

---

*Some Stranraer trains travel via Kilmarnock, and you can follow that route by referring to Maps 12,11,10 & 16, but for the purposes of this section of the guide it is assumed that you are journeying via Paisley.

focus is on the Gilmour Street line, a detour to Paisley Canal can be thoroughly recommended, especially to those who enjoy exploring railway backwaters and lost canals: the former will relish encountering Corkerhill, the G&SWR motive power depot, still very much alive and engaged in diesel maintenance; the latter will enjoy crossing White Cart Water upon an original canal aqueduct variously attributed to Telford or Rennie.

Playing leapfrog with the M8 motorway, the railway strides westwards away from the city centre. Bellahouston Park was the scene, in 1938, of Glasgow's Empire Exhibition, a resounding success. Ibrox football stadium requires little introduction, save to say that it is the work of Archie Leitch, most celebrated of football stadia designers. The branch to Govan was an early vicitim of competition with Glasgow's dense network of electric tramways, but it continued to be busy with goods trains serving the docks and the shipyards until the nineteen-sixties. Cardonald junction now provides access to a rail-freight depot at Deanside, but in earlier days it was the point at which a branch of the Glasgow & Paisley Joint set off for Renfrew before passenger services were abandoned in 1926.

Beyond the Hillingtons, East and West, there are views of the Kilpatrick Hills on the north bank of the River Clyde. Sadly, the avenue of dockyard cranes which formerly accompanied the river have mostly disappeared. Negotiating a sequence of rocky cuttings - there was a tunnel here when the line was first built - the train reaches Paisley's eastern outskirts. Scant evidence remains of Arkleston Junction and the branch to Renfrew, even though it only closed in 1967. This line was adapted, incidentally, from the Paisley & Renfrew Railway of 1837 laid to the 'Scotch' gauge of 4ft 6ins.

Paisley's scintillating skyline has your head twisting back and forth to take it all in. Crossing White Cart Water ('Where Cart rins rowin to the sea'*) there is a broadside view of the Abbey, followed by the high clocktower of the Town Hall, before you are swallowed up by GILMOUR STREET, one of half a dozen stations to have carried the prefix 'Paisley' down through railway history. Gilmour Street marks the end of the G&PJ, and its four platforms are separated into pairs for the Ayr/Largs (G&SWR) and Gourock/Wemyss Bay (CR) lines respectively. Elevated above street level, the station is approached off County Square through a Tudoresque gateway which dates back to its origins in 1840. Up at rail level, however, the effect is a 'strawberry cheescake' extravaganza of finely glazed waiting rooms and offices dating from the quadrupling of the line to Glasgow and reputedly the work of James Miller. First ScotRail's Customer Services Centre here monitors 130 stations in the west of Scotland via CCTV. The dwell time at Gilmour Street is far from sufficient to permit even the slenderest grasp of Paisley's railway history. A glance at the accompanying map hints at something of its past complexity. No less than three separate lines ran to Barrhead (see also Map 12); one belonging to the Glasgow & South Western, the other two to the Caledonian. Constructed between the end of the 19th Century and the beginning of the 20th, at a time of considerable growth in population, the rival companies assumed that the expanding suburbs would be theirs for the taking. But in the event, it was the electric tramways that captured the market for local travel. The Sou' Western route - which had briefly hosted a circular service to and from St Enoch, employing the Canal line in one direction and the Glasgow & Kilmarnock Joint in the other - perished in fits and starts before the First World War. The Caley circuit, from Paisley St James via Ferguslie, Stanely, Barrhead New (reversal), and Dykebar to Paisley East (beyond which a

* The Gallant Weaver- Robert Burns

Paisley Gilmour Street

junction was never laid to the main line) was fully constructed but never provided with a passenger service. Paisley East was demolished to make way for a cinema in 1928, perhaps one of its first features was Buster Keaton in *The Great Locomotive Chase*. Amazingly, the lines retained goods traffic up until the 1960s: Cadburys had a depot at Potterhill and there were textile mills at Gleniffer to the south; there was also an oil terminal at Hawkhead, and a gasworks at Barrhead South (Map 12). Charmingly evocative photographs taken by W. A. C. Smith appear in *An Illustrated History of Glasgow's Railways* (Irwell Press 1995) depicting superannuated Caledonian 0-6-0s trundling along these all but forgotten lines in the 1950s. But perhaps the most unforseen use of the lines in latter days was to effect the delivery of new rolling stock from Pressed Steel at Linwood, notably Glasgow's famous 'Blue Trains', and a whole generation of diesel multiple units. Another traffic from Linwood consisted of tens of thousands of Hillman Imps from the Rootes car plant.

Long before you have digested Paisley's rich railway and industrial roll call, the train will be speeding you away from Gilmour Street beneath the inspired backdrop of the small-domed Coats Observatory, the large-domed Neilson Institute, and the magnificent flying-buttressed Coats Memorial Church. The line from Paisley Canal came in at ELDERSLIE whose paired island platforms are long gone, though a welcome development has seen the introduction of short-haul container trains from Grangemouth operated by DRS (Map 1). Elderslie lays claim to being the birthplace, around 1270, of the Scottish freedom fighter William Wallace. A burrowing junction once offered fast access to the Lochwinnoch/Kilbirnie Loop and Greenock Princes Pier lines, but you would be hard pressed to spot any remains from a train in motion before JOHNSTONE makes its presence felt.

Frosty morning, Lochwinnoch

VEERING south-west through the Lochwinnoch Gap (which would have borne the Ardrossan Canal) the railway finally begins to extricate itself from the greater Glasgow conurbation; though despite the rural quality of its name, MILLIKEN PARK remains steadfastly urban: hard to credit the existence of coal pits hereabouts in the 19th Century, a mainstay of the canal trade.

On the far bank of Black Cart Water (which has its confluence with the White Cart at Renfrew, before the pair pour out into the Clyde a mile downstream) stands the picturesque old weaving village of Kilbarchan, erstwhile easternmost terminus of Glasgow's tramway system, an astonishing 23 miles removed from its counterpart at Airdrie. H. V. Morton elegiacally described the twilight era of Kilbarchan's handloom tartan weavers in his 1933 travelogue *In Scotland Again*.

By HOWWOOD, however, there is a palpable sense of open country. What appears to be a folly on an adjacent hillside celebrates this welcome change in circumstance, though in fact it was a hunting tower from which guests of the McDowalls of long vanished Castle Semple could view chases in the deer park.

To the east a sequence of wooded ridges accompany the line; to the west lie North Ayrshire's peculiarly nameless braes. Half a dozen miles to the north-west, lie the remains of one of Scotland's most unusual railways, a two foot gauge network of light railway lines laid across Duchal Moor. The system was built in 1922 by a shipping magnate to provide access to the grouse shooting. Two of its petrol driven locomotives were refugees from Gretna's munitions plant.

The Black Cart issues from Castle Semple Loch upon which, in ice-bound winters past, generations of Paisley curlers enjoyed their sport. Nowadays the loch plays host to watersports and birdwatching, being incorporated within the Muirshiel Country Park. The late Lochwinnoch Loop Line also plays a recreational role now. Clearly defined by its earthworks, it was built by the Glasgow & South Western Railway in 1905 at the zenith of rail transport when the route between Johnstone and Dalry was virtually full to capacity. In this respect it echoed the London & North Western Railway's Micklehurst Loop in Lancashire's Tame Valley east of Manchester. Embracing contemporary practice, the Lochwinnoch (aka Kilbirnie) Loop was characterised by grade separated junctions to avoid conflicting movements

where it left and rejoined the main line, and island-platformed wayside stations. Less modern in outlook were the bridges in the grounds of the Castle Semple Estate, elaborately castellated to harmonise with the adjacent mansion. Sustrans have brought new life to the Loop Line by adapting it as part of their Carlisle-Glasgow National Cycle Route, No.7. The last real train ran along the route in 1966, but should you pedal furiously enough it is not without the bounds of possibility that you will be transmogrified into a Whitelegg Baltic powering down to catch a sailing from Fairlie Pier.

While Lochwinnoch station on the Loop Line was in existence, the halt on the main line was renamed Lochside to avoid confusion. Between here and Glengarnock you leave Renfrewshire behind and enter Ayrshire. All trace of Glengarnock's once vast iron and steelworks has disappeared following a slow lingering death in the 1970s. Similarly erased is the Lanarkshire & Ayrshire branch from Giffen. A burn runs beneath the platform at GLENGARNOCK station which has all the appearances of being unstaffed until you locate a tiny ticket-hole in one gable end. Knee-deep in slurry, cattle graze disconsolately amidst the remaining earthworks and girder bridgework at the site of Brownhills Junction.

THE great thing about the past is that there is so much of it: multi-layered, it often leaves the one-dimensional present wanting: wanting in atmosphere, wanting in character, wanting in self-belief. Once upon a time they made iron and steel in the Garnock Valley; now they manufacture vitamin supplements - the huge DSM (formerly Roche) plant at which this happens dominates the view beyond abandoned bings as the train approaches Dalry. Sidings with shiny rails and a branch curving across the river into the works confirm that raw materials arrive by rail. From Swinlees Junction a line once ran to quarries. Indeed, there seems to have been a profusion of mineral railways branching off the main line to serve brickworks, ironstone quarries and coal pits. DALRY (pronounced 'Dal-rye') is an old weaving town, whose broach-spired parish church of St Margaret looms above rooftops across the river from the railway. The remains of a former water tower provide circumstantial evidence of the old route to Kilmarnock: evidence bolstered by a line of electricity poles. This was the original means of reaching Kilmarnock from Glasgow by train, and maintained this exclusivity for thirty years until completion of the Glasgow Barrhead & Kilmarnock Joint (Map 10). Perhaps surprisingly, the line continued to carry through passenger services until 1966, though in latter years it was predominantly used by freight, heavier trains finding the gradients easier. A brief rural interlude follows - prior to its industrialisation in the 19th Century the Garnock Valley was considered a country retreat. There are some gracious properties in the vicinity. Monk Castle is a ruined shell, masked from the railway by woodland. Blair also dates from the 17th Century but continues to be occupied. Closer to the railway, Dalgarven Mill houses the Museum of Ayrshire Country Life.

Twenty-six miles from Glasgow, a rank of rusty sidings heralds KILWINNING, a station whose name the pre-recorded lassie on First ScotRail's Juniper electrics seems curiously disinclined to voice. The station is V-shaped with paired platforms on each of the Ayr and Ardrossan routes, its stone-built office houses a booking hall and a kiosk selling newspapers and snacks. Until 1932 there were rival routes between Kilwinning and Glasgow. The one in use today had belonged to the Glasgow & South Western; that which has disappeared originated as the Caledonian Railway's Lanarkshire & Ayrshire line. Rather surprisingly,

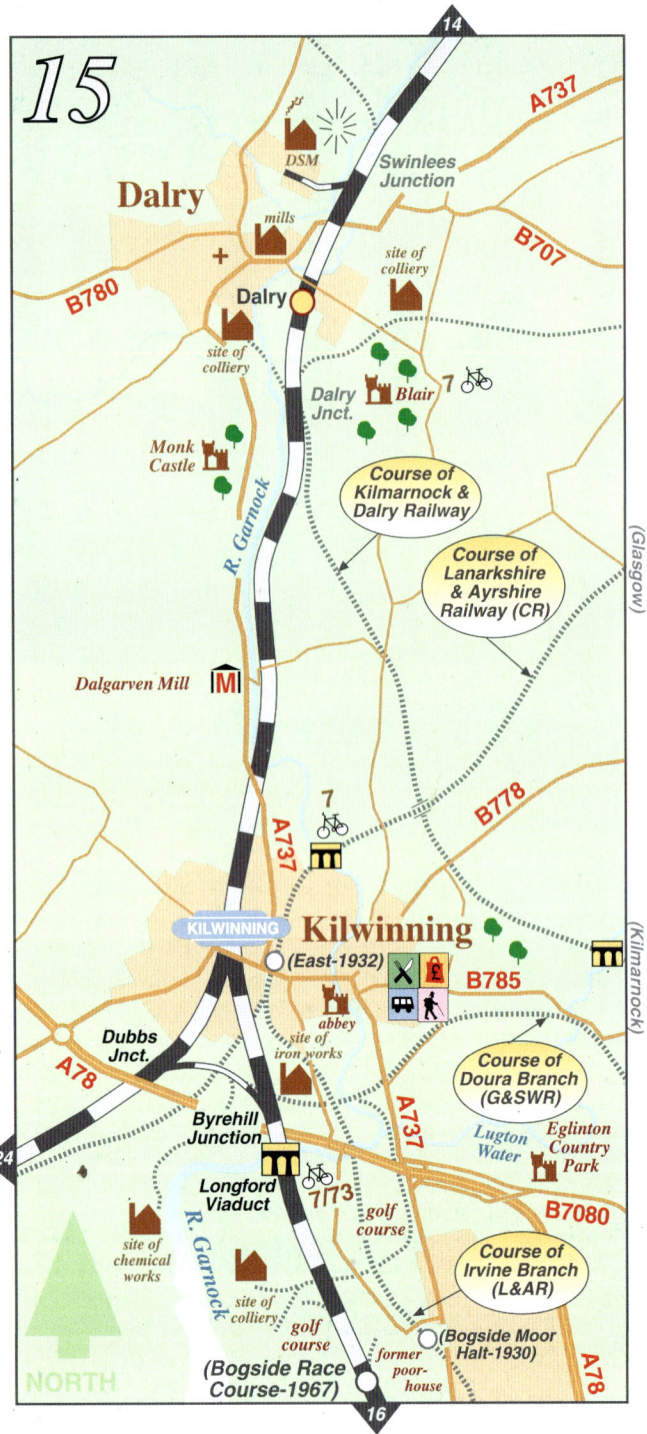

the Caledonian route was the shorter - by half a mile! - but services over it tended to be of a stopping nature as opposed to the Sou' Western's expresses. In 1922 the 9.03am to St Enoch got you into Glasgow forty-four minutes later: leaving eighteen minutes in advance of this service, the 8.45am from the adjacent Caledonian station crossed the Clyde into Glasgow Central four minutes afterwards.

Kilwinning East - as it became known, to avoid confusion, in LMS days - was the junction for the Lanarkshire & Ayrshire route to Irvine Bank Street, very much a branchline byway operated by a one coach shuttle service until passenger services were withdrawn in 1930. The only station en route rejoiced in the name of Bogside Moor Halt, which - in certain vulgar circles - might be considered an amusingly appropriate item of railwayana to have hanging on the door to your smallest room. Another lost line in the vicinity was the Doura Branch which began life as a waggonway carrying coal to Ardrossan. Even after being absorbed by the G&SWR it continued to serve a number of pits in the area as well as Eglinton Iron Works.

Nowadays the electric train for Ayr makes a brisk exit from Kilwinning. At the height of the Depression, however, 'amateur' miners were winning coal from shallow pits beside the line which forced the railway authorities to impose a 5-10mph speed restriction. A patch of grass between housing schemes and some token goal posts mark the course that the Lanarkshire & Ayrshire took in passing beneath the Glasgow & South Western at this point. This is followed by a bus garage and the A78 before your train is carried across the River Garnock as it makes its way out into the Firth of Clyde. Westerly views towards the coast are interrupted by the derelict remains of Nobel's explosives factory (Map 24). Schemes have been floated to have these abandoned acres reclaimed, variously for use as a wind farm, a golf course, or a massive leisure complex. In the meantime, there is a not unattractively surreal beauty to the view.

Four-arched, Longford Viaduct carries the line across the River Garnock. The flood plain here is a nature reserve. Large crowds regularly alighted at BOGSIDE RACE COURSE station, venue for the Scottish Grand National before it was transferred to Ayr after the course's closure in 1965. On the opposite side of the line stands the disused Ravenspark Hospital, formerly Cunninghame Combination Poorhouse.

Mirror image, River Garnock

IRVINE'S old church spires out-soar its new-town environment, but the station surrenders to a nightmare of retail parks and fast food outlets. When the railway first arrived in Irvine the Town Hall clock had to be wound back by seventeen and a half minutes to correspond with Greenwich Mean Time. It would be fun to be able to wind time further back and gain access to the G&SWR's signal works which now lies beneath a McDonalds drive-thru. A brace of disconsolate signal posts and a slice of track struggling out of the undergrowth are all that's left of the line which ran to Kilmarnock via Crosshouse, and which closed in 1964 .

GAILES station served two golf courses - Glasgow Gailes and Western Gailes, both fine links courses if less well known than the likes of Royal Troon. A painting of Western Gailes by G. Drummond Fish adorns the cover of Ian Nalder's book Scotland's Golf in Days of Steam (ISBN 1 84017 034 4) which provides a unique insight into how the development of railways and golf was often intertwined.

The Kilmarnock to Troon line lost its passenger services in 1969, but they were back within half a dozen years, not so much in response to public demand, than because British Rail found it preferable to work through Carlisle-Stranraer services over it rather than via Mauchline and Ayr. By DRYBRIDGE'S abandoned station there is a Standing Stone, shortly after which the train finds itself negotiating a curiously opaque landscape of stunted trees and waving bushes. A rusty track sets hesitantly off into the goblin-haunted purlieus of the neighbouring bog. Old maps are labelled enigmatically with the location of the 'Moss Litter Factory'. Another disused line leads off in the opposite direction towards Hillhouse Quarry, an ungainly landmark on the adjacent hillside. Further to the east lie the ruins of Auchans, the last permanent resident of which was the Countess of Eglinton towards the end of the 18th Century. She was by repute a great beauty who, in her dotage, kept pet rats which were occasionally summoned to dine with her. Crane your neck a little further backwards and you will spot Dundonald Castle, the favourite 14th Century residence of King Robert II, now open to the public under the auspices of Historic Scotland. Where the previous two branch lines are disused, a third, serving the Caledonian Paper Mill on the outskirts of Irvine, remains very much in business, being notably the recipient of one of Britian's lengthiest freight flows, china clay from Cornwall.

Passing beneath the busy A78 trunk road, the train escapes from the discomforting mosslands and finds itself deep in a more reassuringly civilised land of golf links and suburban villas. The Firth of Clyde comes memorably into view as you slow for the junction at Barassie. Once there were vee-shaped platforms serving both routes, but now only stopping trains on the Glasgow line call here. The Glasgow & South Western Railway had its carriage and wagon works at Barassie.

South of Barassie the railway twists seawards to serve Troon. The original route lay inland along what subsequently became known as the Troon Avoiding Line. Taking the opportunity to provide a station nearer the town when it opened the mineral line from Annbank in 1892, the Glasgow & South Western commissioned a Scots architect of growing repute, James Miller, to design a station fit to serve a growing seaside resort. They were generously open minded in giving him the job, for he had previously been employed by the Caledonian. Their trust was not misplaced, for TROON remains one of Scotland's most celebrated stations. A contemporary newspaper report of its opening recorded that a Mr B. Cowan of the British Linen Bank purchased the first ticket, and that 'a fair number of the general public were present to raise a hearty cheer on the arrival of the first train to call, the 5.45am from Ayr to St Enoch.' On a sadder note, many fine steam locomotives were scrapped by the West of Scotland Shipbreaking Co. at Troon Harbour.

Troon

WHEN the world's eight most powerful men landed at Prestwick's 'pure dead brilliant' International Airport in July 2005, they were merrily following in the footsteps of a much more famous man. For it was here, forty-five years earlier, that Elvis Presley made his only foray on to British soil, inadvertently, as it were, during a stop for refuelling made by a US Army transport plane en route for Germany.

Flying at Prestwick dates back to the nineteen-thirties, and there was some wartime activity here too, but it was with the acquisition of the site by the aircraft makers Scottish Aviation that things really took off, so to speak. The massive Palace of Engineering was purloined from Glasgow after the Empire Exhibition of 1938. Eventually SA went into liquidation, but British Aerospace continued to build planes at Prestwick until 1998. Due to a geological anomaly, Prestwick is just about the only aerodrome in the UK guaranteed to be devoid of fog at all times, and in recent years it has enjoyed a renaissance with the advent of budget airlines. Ryanair fly from here to over a dozen tempting destinations, but it would be out of character for you not to remain on the train, faithful to the flanged wheel and South-west Scotland. Aviation fuel is railed in from Grangemouth on a regular basis to a siding on the site of Monkton station. There is no obvious trace, from the train any rate, of the Monkton & Annbank line. It was only ever used by mineral traffic, there once being several coal mines in the area.

But by now golf will be the cynosure of your gaze, and no ordinary golf either, for Prestwick's main golf course proudly lays claim to being the birthplace of Open Golf, the first Championship having been held here on these links on 17th October 1860: there were just eight entrants. The players teed off at noon and had completed all thirty-six holes before darkness fell - and this in October. Willie Park of Musselburgh was the winner with a score of 174, two shots ahead of Old Tom Morris, who won it the following year. The Open went on to be held at Prestwick twenty-four times. On the last occasion in 1924 the railway ran enough excursions to carry fifteen thousand eager spectators to Prestwick to see the tournament won by Jim Barnes. First ScotRail, it must be said, take equal trouble to ensure that present-day golfing fans are conveyed with ease and comfort when the Open takes place north of the border. The first tee lies alongside the up platform, and it is not unknown for tyros to be fazed by

the attention of onlookers in passing trains.

Without the arrival of the railway in 1849, neither PRESTWICK, nor its golf courses, would have developed so readily. In Glasgow & South Western days golfers were offered return tickets between Glasgow and Prestwick for five shillings. No such concession was available to non golfers, though presumably it was eminently possible to sling a spurious bag of clubs across your shoulder to qualify for the lower fare; unless, that is, the terms & conditions demanded that you demonstrate your prowess with a sweet nine iron chip across the concourse at St Enoch.

PRESTWICK'S current station buildings date from 1903; they are single storey and not unpicturesque, though not, of course, in the same class as Troon. Between 1888 and 1901, Prestwick was the recipient of the Glasgow & South Western Railway's only 'slip-coach' operation, described as follows by a local minister of literary bent: "The Glasgow merchants who sojourn here do not need to be told of the excellence of the 4.15pm from the 'Second City' which comes down at full speed, stopping only at Paisley, and by an ingenious method, when in rapid motion, disengaging its latter part at Irvine."

Incongruously, golf gives way to rail freight, specifically Falkland Yard, where long rakes of coal hoppers are stabled pending orders to load imported coal at Hunterston or open-cast Ayrshire coal at one or other of half a dozen loading points in the vicinity. This, then, is the point of origin of all those coal trains which keep the line between Kilmarnock and Carlisle so busy. EWS take the lion's share of the business and the signposted injunction 'No Idling' on their bothy at Falkland seems more directed at their staff's work ethic than the excessive running of engines. Though most of the coal handled here travels long distances to power stations in Yorkshire and the English midlands, a small proportion goes down the harbour branch for export to Ireland. Indeed the Port of Ayr remains reasonably busy, timber being a significant cargo, along with scrap metal, fertilizer, animal feeds, rock salt and, of all things, seaweed. Ayr also regularly features as a port of call for cruise liners, whilst throughout the summer season the paddle steamer *Waverley* is a weekly visitor.

A high proportion of the coal trains use the Mauchline line which curves away from Newton-on-Ayr overlooked, not only by the EWS depot which occupies the site of Ayr engine shed (27F/30C/67C), but also the Somerset Park ground of Ayr

United Football Club whose main stand, opened in 1924, was the work of the celebrated football stadium designer Archibald Leitch. In 1895 a spark from a passing steam train almost set the ground alight, something that few Ayr sides have managed to do since, but at least they have one of football's most memorable nicknames, 'The Honest Men': Burnsian by derivation, naturally.

The River Ayr, having risen (see also Map 9) on the moors above Muirkirk, neatly slices its eponymous county in half. The derivation of its name shares roots with the Yorkshire Aire, and can be defined as 'strong river'. Crossing it by train on the approach to Ayr station, you can look down on its passage out into the Firth of Clyde, catching a glimpse (beyond an early twentieth century cast iron footbridge) of the town's iconic Auld Brig which inspired Burns' poem *The Brigs of Ayr*.

AYR station mirrors Dumfries and Kilmarnock in its layout of north-facing bays, but here the generally agreeable effect is lent added grandeur by the immediate proximity of a station hotel, designed by Andrew Galloway for the Glasgow & South Western Railway in the manner of a French chateau in 1886. Obviously he must have relished the opportunity to let his imagination soar free after a life spent designing engine sheds and other less extravagant structures. It remains an impressive building, florid in its four storeys of deep red sandstone, though apparently more favoured by large touring groups of Scandinavian golfers now than the monied Glaswegian magnates of its heyday. In 1951 it became the first of the G&SWR's four station hotels to pass out of railway ownership.

Leaving the overhead wires of the electrified route from Glasgow astern at Townhead carriage sidings, the railway climbs steeply out of Ayr, threading its way through not always entirely salubrious suburbs before crossing the A77 by-pass at the site of Alloway Junction. This was installed in 1906 when the delightfully named Maidens & Dunure Light Railway was opened to create a coastal route to Girvan which would serve the Glasgow & South Western Railway's magnificent new hotel at Turnberry. Very much a tourists' line, and as such perhaps ahead of its time, it became known as the 'Golfers' Railway'. G&SWR cart-horse manure was used to enhance the fairways of the Turnberry course.

Through trains connected Turnberry with Glasgow St Enoch; the morning's northbound train boasting a Breakfast Car which, upon returning south later in the afternoon transformed itself into a Tea Car. The chameleonic vehicle which provided such exciting fare was a substantial 12 wheeled affair whose bodywork had been built by the G&SWR during the First World War on a Midland Railway underframe dating from 1894. The LMS exiled it to the wilds of the Far North line, but it survived until 1960.

As a scenic railway, the Maidens & Dunure must have surpassed almost anything in the British Isles. Imagine having your kedgeree and kippers served with clifftop views of Arran and the Firth of Clyde thrown in for free. The line's stations were quaint, island-platformed affairs graced by dainty little half-timbered shelters. One need not be a dyed-in-the-wool railway enthusiast to mourn its passing. The LMS Railway's accountants didn't share their predecessor's enthusiasm for the line, irrespective of the bottom line, and closed most of its intermediate stations in 1930; though Turnberry remained accessible from Girvan until 1942. The Ayr end of the line however was revived to serve Billy Butlin's Holiday Camp at Heads of Ayr, a function it fulfilled until 1968, even if its patrons were perhaps less well-heeled and sophisticated than those who once headed so exclusively to James Miller's magnificent caravanserai. In marked contrast to the delights of the M&DLR, an unhappier branch left the Stranraer line just beyond Alloway Junction to serve the Ayr & District Lunatic Asylum at Glengall. At one time visitors were transported into the hospital aboard a Sentinel steam railcar. Coal was still being conveyed along the line to feed the institution's boilers until the early 1960s.

Ornamental ironwork, Ayr

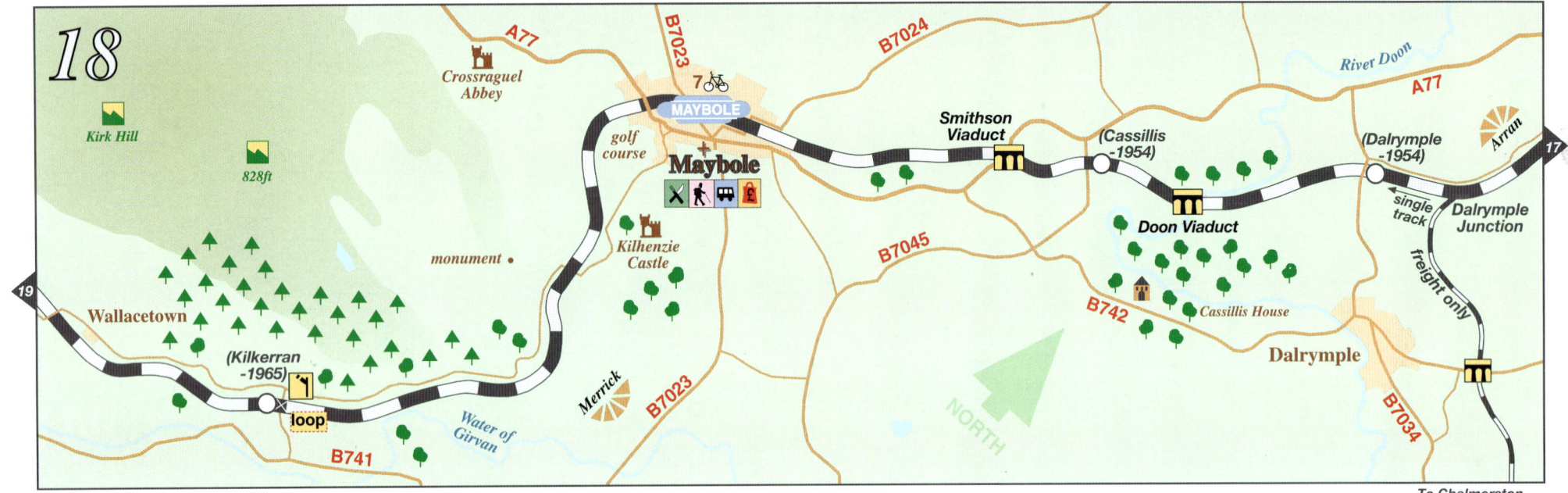

THE line runs double-tracked as far as Dalrymple Junction where a branch which once led to Dalmellington still diverges to serve opencast coal workings along the Doon Valley. The area enjoyed a tradition of iron-making and coal-mining. An extensive network of colliery lines centred on the mine at Waterside and it became a mecca for steam enthusiasts in its final years; many of its locomotives having been built by Barclays of Kilmarnock (Map 10). The Ayrshire Railway Preservation Group, based at Dunaskin, operate steam trains over a short section of the line. Passenger services ceased running to and from Dalmellington in 1964. Nowadays, long trains of coal hoppers, ubiquitously hauled by Canadian built General Motors Class 66 diesel locomotives, come gingerly off the branch with coal, extracted from the shoulders of Benquhat and Benbeoch.

Veering south-westwards, and now single (though once double) track the Girvan line passes the remains of Dalrymple station, closed to passengers in 1954. A delightful interlude follows as the railway runs through woodland and crosses the River Doon, a watercourse which has its source in Loch Enoch, close to Merrick, the highest point of the Galloway Hills, and which pours out into the Firth of Clyde just south of Ayr. Two

or three miles downstream the river reaches Alloway, birthplace of Robert Burns in 1759. Upstream of the railway bridge, though hidden by woodland from the line, lies Cassillis, an ancient house dating back to at least the 14th century. The First Earl of Cassillis, Sir David Kennedy was killed during the Battle of Flodden in 1513. A story concerns one 17th century Lady of Cassillis who had fallen under the amorous spell of the gypsy chief Johnny Faa with whom she planned to elope. The Earl, however, was not prepared to be cuckolded, and forced his wife to watch as he had Faa and his followers hung from trees in the Cassillis parkland. Cassillis station remains in domestic use, whilst its goods yard ironically provides accommodation for a road haulier.

On a clear day, the train offers fine views in a south-easterly direction to a Galloway horizon dominated by the summit of Merrick (2,765ft). The Merrick is the highest hill in the Southern Uplands and is popular with climbers who, on reaching the summit, are rewarded with views as far as the Lake District, Ulster's Mountains of Mourne, and the hills around Crianlarich.

Maybole was the largest - and remains the only open - station between Ayr and Girvan. The Ayr & Maybole Junction

Railway reached here in 1860. Freight came lucratively in footwear; by 1891 Maybole boasted ten factories employing one and a half thousand people producing in the region of a million pairs of boots and shoes per year. But it was a short-lived heyday; one of the largest factories had closed by 1907, causing mass emigration of a significant proportion of the local populace to Canada. The last shoe factory eked out a dwindling trade until being gutted by fire in 1962 - a soul destroying day in the annals of a town which could once lay claim to being the Capital of Carrick.

Only the down platform remains in use. On the up side, overgrown with weeds, the name MAYBOLE remains picked out in whitewashed stone letters as part of what must once have been a pretty station garden. Built of local sandstone, the station building has turned its back on the railway and been born again as a convenience store. The station itself has been reinvented too, as a multi-modal transport centre (MMTC). Over half a million pounds was recently spent to permit it to acquire this status, the bulk of this on a spanking new footbridge fully compliant with the Disability Discrimination Act (DDA). A good deal of the work was undertaken at night; not, as has been suggested, to disguise

the sheer inappropriate ugliness of the new bridge, but to Minimise Disruption to Rail Services (MDRS).

Emerging from cuttings, the line skirts Maybole's nine-hole municipal golf course, overlooked by a war memorial, and makes temporarily for the south-east, as if theoretically uncertain of the way, but in practice simply making for the accommodating valley of the Water of Girvan. To the west you catch a glimpse of the ruins of Crossraguel Abbey, a 13th Century Cluniac monastery. Prominent on a hillside to the west of the railway looms an obelisk erected by public subscription to Sir Charles Ferguson of Kilkerran in 1857. His son, Sir James, is remembered by a statue in Ayr commemorating a busy life between 1832 and 1907, spent variously as a soldiering veteran of the Crimea, an MP for Ayrshire and Manchester, the Postmaster General and Governor of New Zealand, South Australia and Bombay.

Arboreally inclined, the train makes its way through woodland glades of considerable charm which have you thinking of remote branchlines in France or Portugal. Coastal and moorland scenery is what you anticipate between Ayr and Stranraer, but the Water of Girvan valley is every bit as intoxicating.

Kilkerran lost its lonely station in 1965, but its signal box survives, as does the crow-stepped, stone-built station house, headquarters now of a firm manufacturing rounded timber fence poles. North of the level crossing the line bifurcates into a loop protected by semaphore signals, a useful passing point between Ayr and Girvan. The station was erected, not for wizards in these darkling woods, but for the aforementioned Fergusons of Kilkerran. Their mansion lies across the river and dates from the first half of the 18th Century: 'a house of dignity and much charm in a fairytale setting' according to Rob Close in his most enjoyable and fascinating *Ilustrated Architectural Guide to Ayrshire & Arran* - RIAS 1992 ISBN 1873190 06 9. Gradually it dawns on you that this valley is peculiarly full of big houses embowered in gracious parkland.

Ferguson monument, Maybole

SWITCHBACK gradients, long shut stations, abandoned mines; all this and more as the train runs exhilaratingly through the forest like a herd of deer. Gracious policies there may be, throughout the valley of the Water of Girvan, but that could not prevent it becoming a centre for coal mining for five hundred years. As early as the 16th century, Acts of Parliament were being passed forbidding the export of coal on account of its scarcity. The earliest record of coal mining in the Girvan Valley relates to a licence granted by the monks of Crossraguel Abbey in 1415. Since then over a hundred sites relating to coal extraction by one means or another have been charted. In 1835 a miner was trapped in Kilgrammie Pit for twenty-three days, only to die three days after being rescued. John Brown by name, his gravestone is to be found in the parish churchyard at Dailly.

The mid-19th century advent of the railway revolutionised the transport of coal out of the valley, but by that time more sophisticated methods of mining were concentrating work on a handful of pits. Largely surrounded by woodland now, it is difficult to accept that some of these mines survived into the 20th century. Killochan Mine, also known as Bargany Pit, remained in business until 1967, Maxwell, amazingly, until 1973. Often, the daily coal train northwards out of Killochan was heavy enough to require double heading. Apparently there was a wayside halt in the woods for the benefit of travelling miners. Black cattle now graze between the boles of silver birch on the site of Killochan Mine.

Beautiful as the woodlands are, they all but prevent views of the valley's most handsome properties. One thinks especially of Dalquharran Mansion, only briefly glimpsed from the train, despite commanding an enviable position overlooking the adjacent riverbank. No less an architect than Robert Adam built it in 1785, for his niece and her husband, Thomas Kennedy. Aesthetically, it has been ranked above Culzean Castle on the coast, yet now lies reproachfully empty, turning blind eyes across the valley, cheek by jowl beside the ruined fortification of Dalquharran Castle. Some, however, might argue that their fate is preferable to that of Brunston Castle which has become a luxury holiday complex and golf course.

Killochan station has been closed for half a century and more. On the down side the station house is domestically occupied, the old waiting room, copiously glazed, a derelict extension displaying lost dignity. Killochan Castle dates from the 16th century, a tower house with conically roofed turrets.

Passing an industrial estate dominated by William Grant's distillery, the line reaches the outskirts of GIRVAN. An embankment marks the former entry of the Maidens & Dunure Light Railway on its coastal journey down from Turnberry. The Maybole & Girvan Railway opened for traffic in 1860, terminating at a station across the Girvan Water from which a line continued to the harbour to facilitate trade between sea and rail. This station remained in use for seventeen years pending extension of the line southwards to Stranraer. Thereafter it continued to be used as the town's goods depot. The late Derek Cross, one of Scotland's foremost railway photographers, had an idyllic photograph published on the cover of *Railway World* in 1967 depicting a 'Crab' 2-6-0 shunting across the timber bridge which carried the line across the river to its original terminus.

Girvan's present station looks as if it has escaped from a Hornby-Dublo train set circa 1955. This is a not entirely spurious assumption, for it is indeed a Fifties design, having been built to replace the previous station buildings burnt down in 1946. To present eyes its oozes

Token gossip, Girvan

Tunnel vision, Girvan

retro charm. Staffed until early afternoon, you can wander through the booking hall imagining yourself fresh from a day on Girvan's sands, suffering inwardly from a surfeit of Italian ice cream and fish supper. Opposite the ticket office the blind stays permanently down on what must once have been the station newsagents counter. The platforms are connected by a tiled subway reached via stairs framed by soberly - as reflects the austere post-war period - ornate metal railings.

The drivers of trains proceeding southwards collect a token in a hooped pouch from the signalman whose box stands at the south end of the up platform. When they planned to link Girvan to Stranraer, the Victorian railway builders had a choice of going round via the coast or across the moors. The coastal route, though shorter, would have necessitated expensive rock-blasting and been prone to storm damage and erosion. With this in mind, the inland proposal won the day, though not without misgivings, for the route would entail formidable earthworks and switchbacking gradients. Such gradients are immediately apparent as the train leaves Girvan on a taxing 1 in 54 and climbs through a deep cutting beneath the gorse-rich slopes of Dow (pronounced 'Doo') Hill. Only the low speed and increased exertions of today's under-floor-engined diesel units hint at the steepness of the ascent, but back in steam days the often double-headed boat trains would require all the experience and ingenuity of their footplate crews to be coaxed up to the summit at Milepost 4. Still climbing, the train emerges from Glendoune Cutting to be met by one of the most dramatic views on Britain's rail network, the spectacular sight of Ailsa Craig, ten miles out to sea in the Firth of Clyde. Over a thousand feet high, and two miles in circumference, this huge granite island is the plug of an extinct volcano. Once it was inhabited and celebrated for the quality and durability of its curling stones. Now it is noted for its gannets.

Early morning walk, Pinwherry

BREASTING the summit, the train runs under the afternoon shadows of Byne Hill with its dramatic outcrops of rock, and skirts Balaclava Wood as it twists to face south-east and the portal of Pinmore Tunnel. Glendrissaig Reservoir, fished by the Carrick anglers now, was a landmark for footplate crews in the steam era. If they got that far they considered themselves safely on their way. Heavier trains were banked up from Girvan to the summit, whereupon they were meant to voice a farewell whistle and drop back down the line, but there were over enthusiastic crews on the bankers who believed in giving the train an extra shove over the summit, much to the irritation of the train locomotive's crew who would by then be concentrating on safely negotiating the convoluted descent to Pinwherry.

Embankments and cuttings create an easier passage for the railway compared to the adjacent A714 road which corkscrews with the contours. Above the tunnel lies Dinvin Motte, a prehistoric fort. By the time daylight returns at the far end of Pinmore's quarter of a mile long tunnel the road has swapped sides. PINMORE station had a passing loop but only one platform face. The whitewashed station building remains intact and in domestic use. The road crosses the line again as the latter negotiates a rocky cutting on the approach to Kinclair Viaduct, an imposingly curved, eleven arch masonry structure, much photographed in the past by the likes of Derek Cross and W.V.J. Anderson but nowadays difficult to get an angle on owing to private land and increased tree cover.

The River Stinchar enters from the east, having flowed down off the Galloway Hills. Nestling almost beneath a small, three arch viaduct, Pinmore's isolated church predates the railway by some forty years. Originally it belonged to the Episcopalian faith and a priest from Girvan would travel out to take services. Incumbents must have welcomed the opening of the railway. After a period of disuse in the 20th century it is in use again under the auspices of the Celtic Church, with services being held on the last Sunday of each month.

The original Laggansarroch Viaduct was demolished by a freak storm in 1875 before the line had even opened. It had been a conventional masonry structure, but its replacement is of iron. Beyond it the right hand side of the train offers views down the Stinchar Valley dominated in the distance by the sugar-loaf summit of Knockdolian. The Stinchar runs

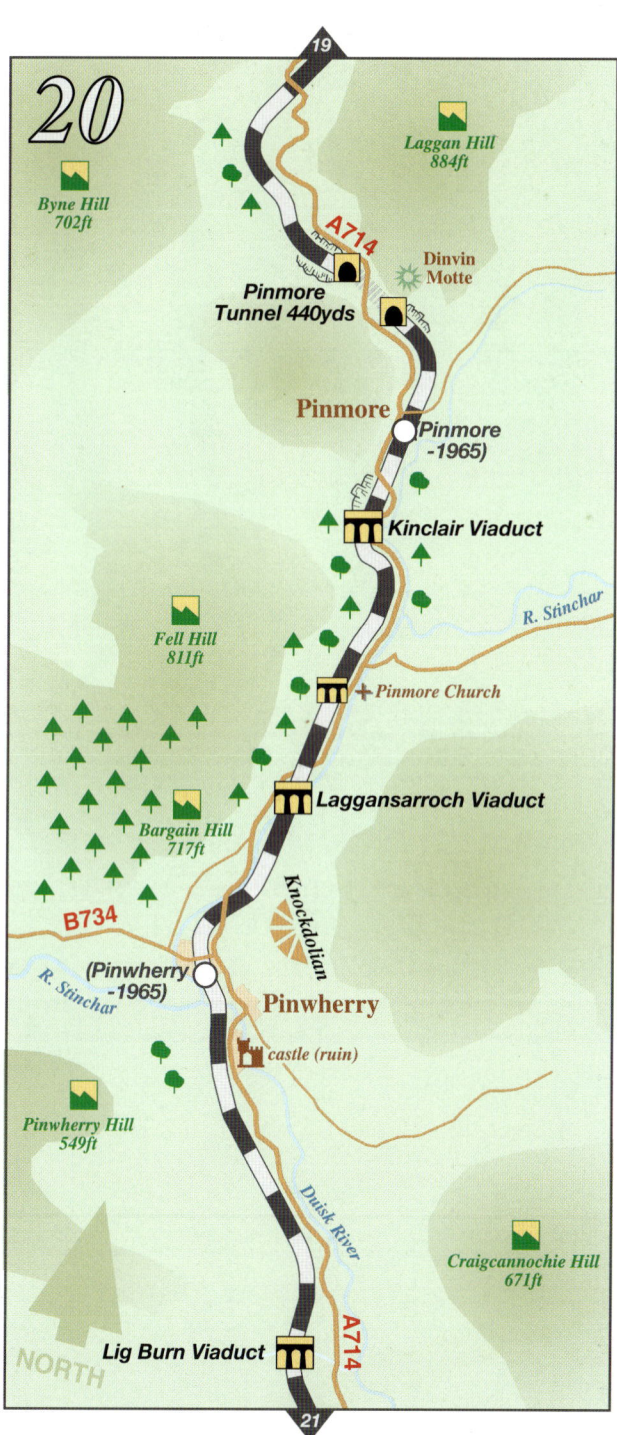

down to the coast at Ballantrae. Once a lawless haunt of smugglers, by the end of the 19th century its fishing industry was booming. Both the Glasgow & South Western and Caledonian railway companies had goods agents in Ballantrae, the former routeing their fish on horse-drawn wagons to Girvan, the latter taking its share down the coast to Stranraer. In due course of railway time both consignments would reach London's Billingsgate fish market. Such was the level of trade that several schemes were mooted to take a branch down the Stinchar Valley, the last as late as 1918. Incidentally, Bennane Head, just up the coast from Ballantrae, was the home, during the 16th century, of Sawney Bean and his outlaw band of cannibalistic cave dwellers. They were thought to have killed and eaten up to a thousand victims in their time, but in due course met their just desserts, being captured and taken to Edinburgh where they were bled to death for their troubles.

The line curves round past the site of PINWHERRY station which closed in 1965, though a loop, overlooked by a signal box, remained in use until 1992. The Stinchar is joined by Duisk Water here and the line crosses the latter on a skew bridge overlooked by a former creamery and a ruined castle. Pinwherry featured in Dorothy L. Sayers *Five Red Herrings* detective novel in which her aristocratic sleuth, Lord Peter Wimsey, sought to solve a murder amongst Galloway's artistic community. Unlike many fiction writers, Sayers did a fair degree of homework with contemporary railway timetables and working practices to authenticate the plot of this 1931 novel. Embarrassingly all too often this isn't the case, with protagonists leaving Euston for York or St Pancras for Ely to name but two ill advised examples.

Beyond Pinwherry the line begins climbing again, up the Duisk Valley in this instance, through pastureland largely given over to sheep rearing. Neat little farms sprinkle the countryside which has a well kept air about it. The dense forestry plantations of Galloway form a distant horizon in which the Merrick is again prominent. At its steepest the ascent to Barrhill is a gruelling 1 in 73. When the Glasgow & South Western Railway operated this line between 1892 and 1923, it was company policy for locomotive crews to take it easy uphill so as to conserve fuel, then to speed downhill to keep to the schedule.

WHEN the Girvan & Portpatrick Junction Railway was being promoted, its supporters had a clear vision of their objective, which was to reach Stranraer. They harboured few illusions that there would be any intermediate traffics in the offing; some cattle to be moved, perhaps, but precious little else. No, the *raison d'etre* for the G&PJR was to shorten considerably the railway route between Glasgow and the port for Northern Ireland, Stranraer. Prior to completion of the link between Girvan and Challoch Junction to the east of Stranraer, travellers from Glasgow had initially to go to Dumfries where they would change into a train running over the Portpatrick & Wigtownshire Railway via Castle Douglas and Newton Stewart, a total distance of 155 miles. When the Girvan & Portpatrick Junction opened in 1877 it sliced a third of the distance off that roundabout journey at one stroke. How ironic, then, that this is now the only railway link to Stranraer. Marples and Beeching (direct heirs to the Vaudeville traditions of Hitler and Goebbels), wanted to do away with both routes, calculating that the Ayr line was losing £66k annually. They recommended that express buses could replace the boat trains, but failed to reveal that it would cost £530k to upgrade the A77 to a suitable standard to operate such vehicles.

You may mull over such paradoxes and perversities of railway history as the train climbs towards Barrhill, southern outpost of Strathclyde Passenger Transport territory, and sole intermediate station left open between Girvan and Stranraer. Down in the valley of the Duisk River stands a big house called Kildonan, completed in 1923 by the architect James Miller who, you will remember, also designed many items of railway architecture including Troon station and the Turnberry Hotel for the Glasgow & South Western Railway. Kildonan has been referred to as 'the last great country house in the Gothic Revival tradition', but in spite of such praise it was probably too grand for its setting and too late in the day to do itself justice; in the English Cotswolds it might just have worked, in this lowland Scottish wilderness it was an anachronism. The completed building, which took almost a decade to build, included indoor tennis courts and a theatre. Nowadays it caters for holiday rentals and bed & breakfast and also houses a restaurant.

BARRHILL lies remotely the best part of a mile above and beyond the riverside village it is named after. The line

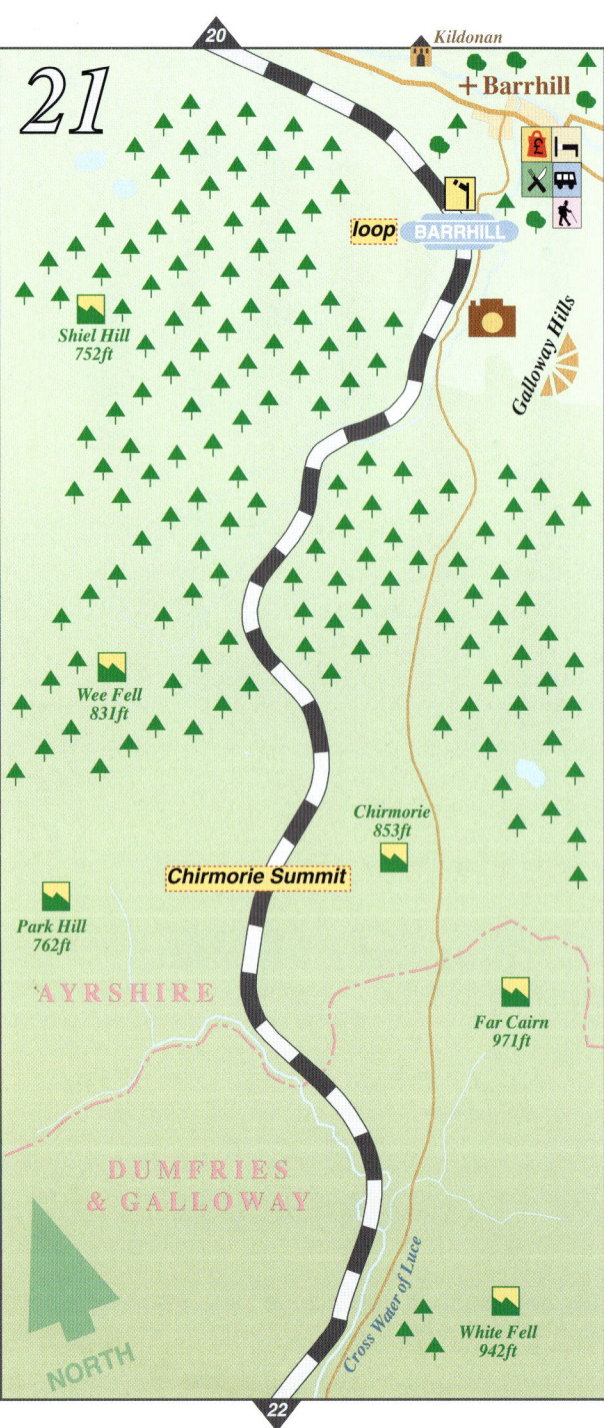

bifurcates into a loop with up and down platforms. The diminutive sentry-box like signal cabin was brought here, surplus to requirements from Portpatrick in the Thirties following the destruction by fire of its predecessor. There isn't room in the cabin for anything other than the lever-frame, so the token equipment (marvellous Tyer's patent machinery immaculately kept) is located in the station building. In steam engine days Barrhill was the only point at which water could be taken between Girvan and Stranraer. Signalling here must be a lonely occupation, and so it is not surprising to see the signal man or woman snatching a welcome moment of gossip or the odd joke or two with passing drivers as they exchange tokens for the sections to Girvan or Glenwhilly. Passengers seem few and far between, even though the occasional bus offers connections to and from Newton Stewart.

Relentlessly, the railway continues to climb from Barrhill at an intimidating 1 in 67. Briefly the landscape is one of bare moorland, predominantly grazed by sheep, and there are wonderful views eastwards towards the Galloway Hills again. But then suddenly you are engulfed by forestry and you cease to feel yourself so much in Scotland as in Central Europe; the Harz Mountains perhaps, or even further east in the Carpathians. The Scottish Executive are providing a grant of over five million pounds for the development of a railhead, to be served by custom-built freight multiple units with built-in cranes, which will enable timber to be extracted without the use of lorries on local roads. It is expected that 110,000 tonnes per annum will be railed from Barrhill: to Ayr, Troon, Carlisle, and Chirk in North Wales.

Emerging from the trees, the line reaches its summit at Chirmorie, 690 feet above sea level. Once there were surfacemen's cottages here, built for the workers who maintained the track. On Fridays, according to David L. Smith, an express stopped to carry the men's wives down to Stranraer to do their shopping. Crumbling snow fences accentuate the eerie nature of this windswept setting, as the moors stretch out for miles into the distance like a transmogrified sea. Downgrade now, the railway crosses the boundary between what was once Ayrshire and what what was once Wigtownshire. The burns beside the line are flowing southwards, and yet you are still only halfway between Girvan and Stranraer!

The Way through the Woods, Barrhill

Wind-bent Hawthorn, Glenwhilly

LIKE a fine, but not particularly well known, wine which appeals to certain sophisticated palates, the railway which crosses the bare moors of Galloway has its own exclusive fan base, connoisseurs of its austere and underestimated beauty. These disciples are easy to differentiate from other travellers because their gaze is forever focussed beyond the carriage window as if savouring the line's unique bouquet. Fellow travellers seem less appreciative, slumped over reading matter or talking in Ulster accents which only appear to have one level of volume - loud!

Mileposts - to the west of the line - measure the distance from Girvan. No.20 precedes GLENWHILLY. Once, believe it or not, there was a wayside station here, together with a siding where cattle and sheep could be loaded. Now there is just a lonely loop and an equally lonely signalman. It is hard to credit that old photographs depicting the station buildings and the platforms with their neat rows of oil lamps have not somehow been doctored or enhanced. There is no sign now of any building, save for the signal box. From this hermitage the signalman descends to exhange tokens with your driver, a ritual habitually accompanied by wry laughter, as though there were some running joke from box to box; perhaps they are still amused by the discovery of an adder nesting in the toilet some years back. Today's staple diet of two-car diesel units must seem poor fare to the signallers. Their predecessors had to juggle with lengthy trains of a dozen coaches or more. At the next crossing point along the line, New Luce, it was not unknown for trains to be divided and shunted into the goods yard to enable two to pass. Such difficulties were exacerbated by the Second World War and the regular operation of troop trains. Two Highland Railway River Class 4-6-0s were put back into steam to deal with these trains and given the ironic nicknames *Scharnhorst* and *Gneisenau* after the German battleships.

Although it is generally downhill from Chirmorie there is a brief climb at 1 in 70 beyond Glenwhilly as the line is carried over the adjoining moorland on a sizeable embankment. In 1947 a lightweight Glasgow-Stranraer train hauled by a Jubilee Class locomotive became stuck in a snowdrift on this stretch of track. Night had fallen and it was decided to keep the passengers on board rather than attempt to make them trudge back on foot to Glenwhilly. The footplate crew remained in their cab and kept the fire stoked to provide steam heat for the carriages. Consignments of food being carried in the guard's van were requisitioned to provide a meal. Unfortunately the weather failed to improve the next day and the train remained marooned. The locomotive ran out of water and the fire had to be doused. There was no longer any heating or lighting in the carriages and temperatures plummeted. Not until the third day was it possible to rescue the snowbound train's passengers and crew. A train from the Stranraer end had managed to reach the "Swan's Neck" and the passengers, many by now stretcher-bound, were conveyed to it with the help of German prisoners of war still awaiting repatriation. A further two days elapsed before the train was dug out of the snow. It seemed appropriate, somehow, that the locomotive's name was *Defiance*.

Squeaking around the reverse curves of the "Swan's Neck", even diesel units appear to establish a gravitas of sorts, an intimacy with the landscape that is almost profound. The train's horn echoes like a bugle call across the valley and you find yourself descending into a softer, cultivated countryside of pastures and woodland by NEW LUCE. The station here was unusual in that it had staggered platforms.

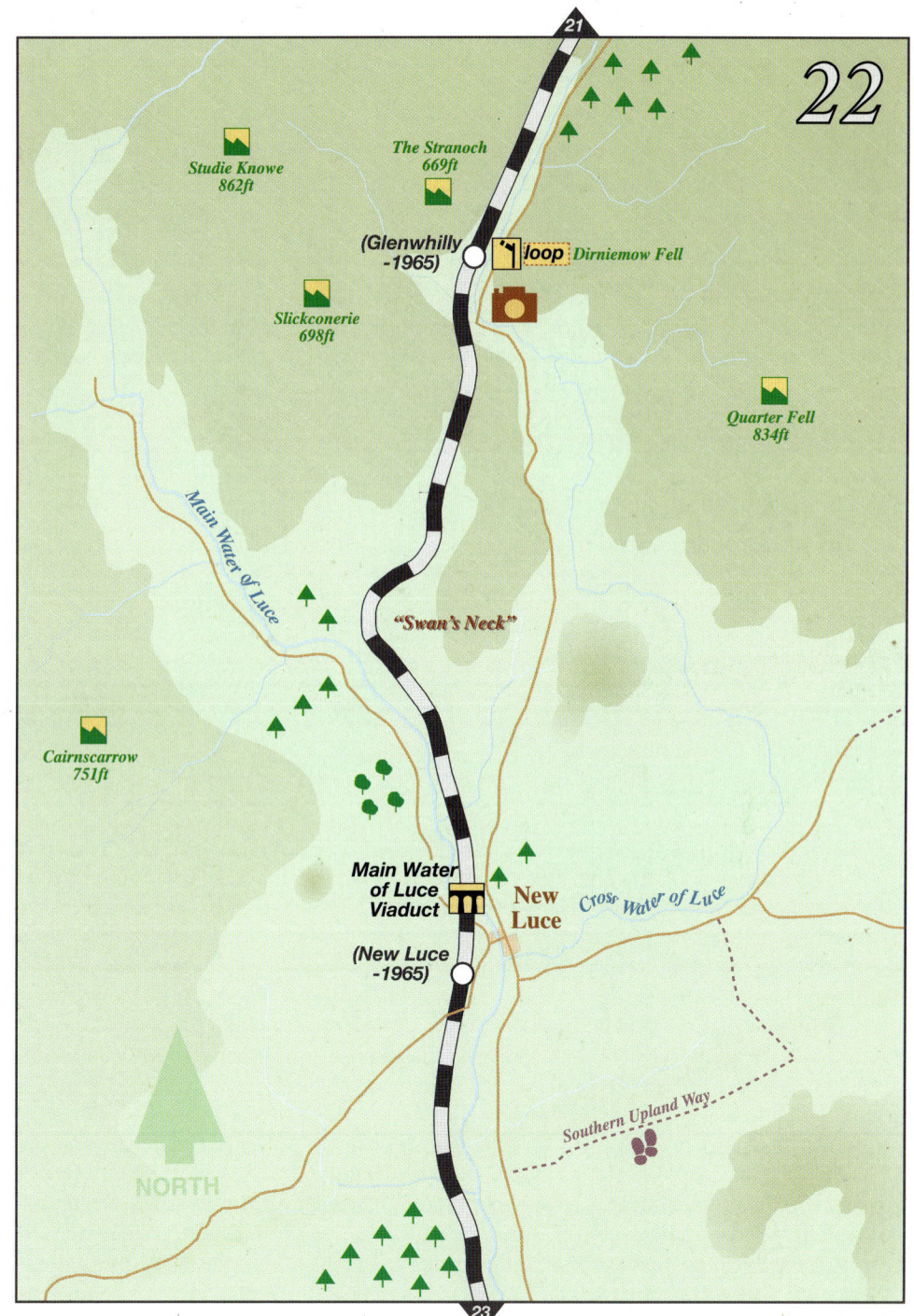

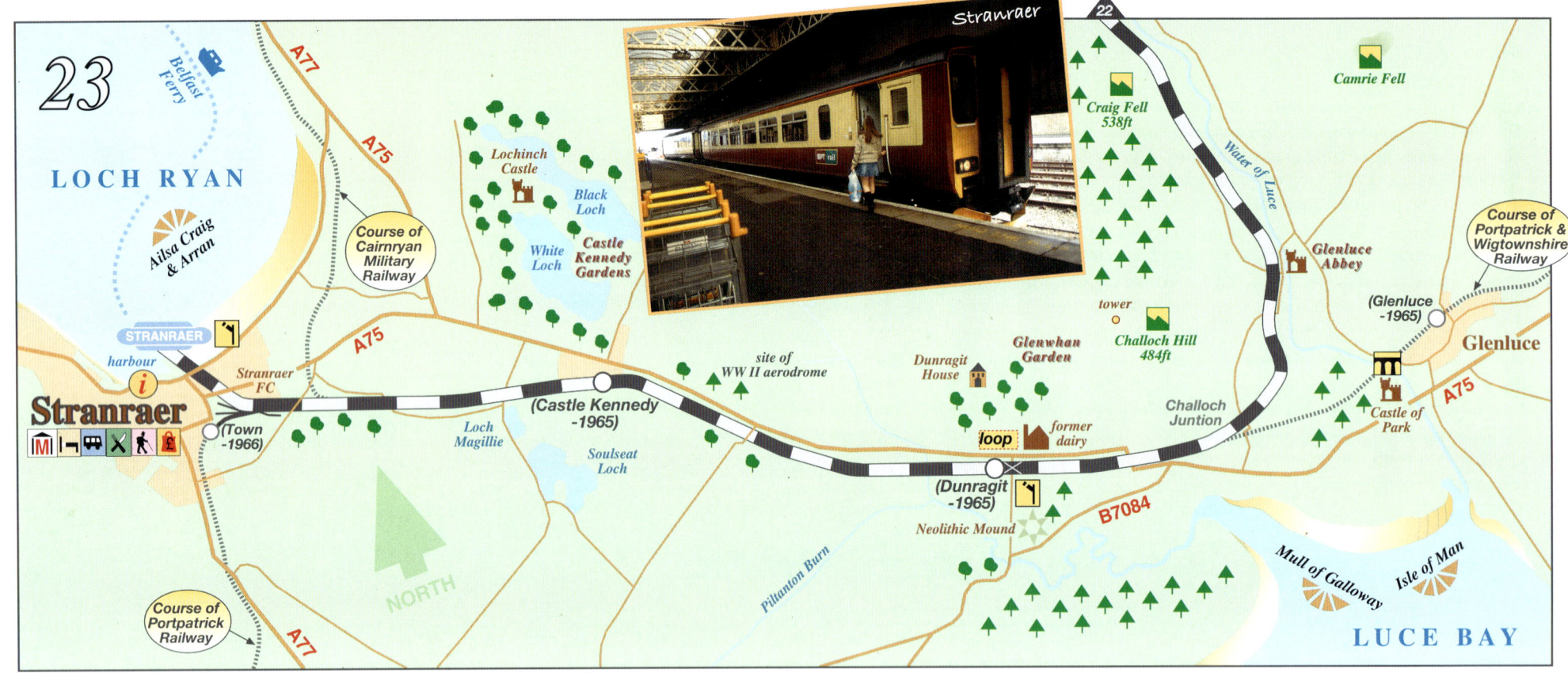

Stranraer

MANY railway journeys, however scenically dramatic they might be somewhere along the line, end in anti-climax, but this one continues to spring some nice surprises right up to its buffer-stops. At Glenluce there are glimpses from the train of an abbey founded for the Cistercians in the 12th Century, though it is only the later Chapter House which remains more or less intact. Previous visitors to the abbey range from Robert the Bruce to Mary Queen of Scots, and now the general public, courtesy of Historic Scotland, can follow in such august footsteps. Also briefly visible, to the south-east, stands the Castle of Park, built by the son of the last Abbot of Glenluce at the end of the 16th Century using some of the abbey's stonework. Nowadays it's leased to the Landmark Trust for holiday accommodation. It must offer an even better view over Luce Bay than the train, certainly one of lengthier duration. In clear conditions the Mull of Galloway is magically

revealed. Even perhaps the Isle of Man; specifically Point of Ayre and Jurby Head, thirty-five miles to the south-east.

Any excitement at such topographic revelations is tempered by the melancholy entrance on to the scene of the trackbed which once carried the direct line into Stranraer from Dumfries, a victim (as you have already perhaps learned and grieved for on Map 4) of the Beeching cuts in 1965. This line was the melodramatic scene in 1930 of Freeman Wills Crofts' detective story *Sir John Magill's Last Journey*, the eponymous hero of which is murdered on the overnight boat train between Euston and Stranraer. Crofts, who gained a teasing mention in Dorothy L. Sayers aforementioned *Five Red Herrings*, was equally at pains to authenticate his railway settings, but then he had inside knowledge, for he had worked as a railway engineer in Ulster. CHALLOCH JUNCTION was created when the Girvan & Portpatrick Junction Railway

opened in 1877, the abandoned line from Dumfries via Castle Douglas and Newton Stewart pre-dated it by sixteen years.

DUNRAGIT lost its station when services ceased over the direct 'Port Road' from Dumfries, but there has recently been talk of re-opening it as a railhead for The Rhins and The Machars; not a bad idea, Rhins & Machars Parkway would roll nicely off the tongue. The whitewashed station house remains intact, even if, the timber built and canopied extension to the west, containing the booking hall, waiting room and parcels office and prominent in archive photographs, has been demolished. David L. Smith has written affectionately of the adjacent cottage where once upon a time an enterprising wife of one of the signalmen dispensed teas in her front parlour. That great chronicler of the Sou' Western changed train here on 5th August 1919 en route from Dalmellington to Whithorn. To his amazement the

3.15pm ex Stranraer hoved into view double-headed by a Caledonian Railway locomotive and one belonging to the Glasgow & South-Western, an unprecedented event in his then still youthful experience. The station may currently be closed, but the signal box remains very much in business, and unique here in Scotland in that a token is exchanged for a tablet. The signalman here may well be much less isolated than his colleague back at Glenwhilly, but he seems to be sharing the same running joke. In 1882 the grandiloquently named Farmers Co-operative Creamery Association opened a large works at Dunragit with its own sidings. In the creamery's heyday some three hundred workers travelled daily by train to the plant from Stranraer. It closed in 1960 though some industrial use of the lineside buildings remains. Far deeper into the past, the Dunragit Mound is a recently excavated Neolithic ceremonial monument which has invited comparison with Silbury Hill in Wiltshire.

Arrow-like, the train leaves the laughing signalman behind, accelerating away on the last lap as if it's privvy to something you're not. In spring the cuttings are ablaze with gorse. In summer lineside fields of maize hint at a kinder climate now that all those creased moorland contours have been ironed out. The mileposts, by the way, are measured from Castle Douglas, as this was previously part of the Portpatrick & Wigtownshire Joint Railway, a not always harmonious collaboration between the Caledonian, Glasgow & South Western, London & North Western and Midland railways.

On the outskirts of CASTLE KENNEDY an aerodrome was opened in 1941 to act as an air gunnery school. After the war it was decommissioned, but briefly enjoyed a new lease of life in the mid-1950s when Silver City Airways operated car ferry flights between here and Newtownards in Ulster and Ronaldsway on the Isle of Man employing Bristol 170s. The aerodrome was merely one of many wartime installations in and around The Rhins. Both the Girvan and Dumfries lines were heavily used by troop trains and additional goods traffic, resulting in the section between Dunragit and Stranraer being doubled, though it is once again single now.

The most significant wartime development was the Cairnryan Military Railway. If you have travelled on the West Highland Line with *Iron Roads to the Isles* for company, you will know of the creation of Military Port No.1 at Faslane in 1943. Its counterpart, Military Port No.2, was opened the same year on the east bank of Loch Ryan and was linked to the main line by a branch just over six miles long. Exchange sidings were laid at the meeting point of the two lines a mile east of Stranraer Town station. To provide accommodation for the workforce half a dozen elderly carriages were requisitioned along with an equally superannuated Highland Railway 4-4-0 *Loch Moy* to provide steam heating. The port's military heyday was brief. Within a year of its commissioning focus had shifted to the south coast of England in preparation for D-Day, though construction work on sections for the Mulberry Harbour ensured that the line remained busy. For a while it boasted a passenger service to carry personnel between the various installations it served and to allow them leisure access to Stranraer, the return fare from Cairnryan being a princely tuppence ha'penney. Archive photographs in the Imperial War Museum collection depict an LNER J50 0-6-0 tank trundling along with a train of six-wheeled carriages providing this service. For some years, during and after the war, milk from Ulster was shipped into Cairnryan and railed to Glasgow. After the war the railway was used to convey redundant munitions for

disposal at sea, and there was trade in scrap metal too in connection with a shipbreaking yard that developed on the site of the port; the aircraft carrier *Ark Royal* being one of its melancholic victims. The line was last used in 1962, though a good deal of its course can still be traced, whilst there have been suggestions that it could usefully be relaid to provide passenger train access to the ferry port at Cairnryan.

The train appears to heave a phlegmatic sigh as it slows for STRANRAER. The town's railway infrastructure has been ravaged since the 1960s, yet a good deal of it obstinately remains in place, *Marie Celeste* like in its apparent refusal to face abandonment permanently. There has been no freight this way since 1994 when steel bound from Scunthorpe to Ireland was sent by road via Heysham instead; though loading ramps and lifting equipment are still reproachfully in place. Stranraer Town station and its neighbouring engine shed (12H/68C/67F) closed in 1966, yet are still eerily intact amidst a sea of rusty sidings. An option for the railway when (and if as planned) the ferry operation moves to Cairnryan in 2007 is to foreshorten the line to terminate at a new station where the road to Cairnryan crosses the line.

Until 1950 you could travel beyond Stranraer to Portpatrick. The latter had been the traditional harbour for the short-sea crossing to Donaghadee in County Down - just over twenty miles away - since the 17th Century. But Portpatrick lay perenially at the mercy of westerly gales and, despite attempts by Smeaton and Rennie to create enclosed harbours, ferry operations moved to the calmer waters of Loch Ryan in 1872, just ten years after the railway to Portpatrick had been completed. With steep gradients and tight curves it had been a difficult line to operate in any case, and for the remainder of its working life it slumbered apologetically on as a railway backwater. Slumbered, that is, until war broke out, and at such a premium was the siding capacity of Stranraer that it became an operating habit to store incoming trains nose to tail along the Portpatrick line until they could be assimilated as appropriate.

Wheels squealing the train approaches its terminus, passing Stair Park, home of Stranraer FC, 'The Blues'. Though founded as long ago as 1870, the club did not gain league status until 1955, there being a barely disguised prejudice by clubs located in the Central Belt against making the lengthy journey down to this remote south-west corner of Scotland. The club's blue and white strip reflects the town's maritime connections. Stair Park has a capacity of six thousand; though crowds rarely rise beyond three figures; obviously that prejudice exists with supporters too.

But such sadnesses are quickly forgotten as the train emerges out on to the lochside setting of Stranraer's Harbour station. Ensure you fix your gaze to the right, and the waters of Loch Ryan, rather than left over lorry-parks. The train slows beneath Pampas Grass and semaphore signals, and the signalman has come down from his sizeable box and crossed the tracks to collect the token; a transaction symbolically greater than the sum of its parts, for this is inescapably journey's end, and the traveller who travels for travel's sake has to weigh up their options before deciding where to go next. You can get to Belfast by boat before you can get back to Glasgow by train. But, on second thoughts, Stranraer deserves your attention too. The gloomy station is not wholly representative of the town it continues to serve. There are echoes here and there of prouder days in the not too distant past when it boasted Sleeper and Motorail services, though it is admittedly more difficult to imagine the scene on 23rd January 1912 when a record catch of herring required the operation of ten special fish trains.

'PICTURE to yourself everlasting bleak sand dunes. Between us and America there is nothing but water, a sea whose mighty waves are always raging and foaming. Without work the place would be intolerable'. This is how Alfred Nobel, writing to his brother, described Ardeer in 1871. The Swedish inventor and munitions magnate was in this remote corner of Ayrshire to set up a factory which, at its zenith, would occupy five square miles of sand dunes and employ thirteen thousand workers. In 1890, the year of Nobel's death - his will included a legacy for the establishment of annual prizes for achievement in the fields of chemistry, physics, medicine, literature and (somewhat ironically) peace - the Glasgow & South Western Railway provided a private station for the workforce which remained in use until 1966. Nowadays, the sidings leading in to the plant are overgrown and rusty, though the site continues to be occupied by a chemical works specialising in the production of nitrocellulose, as used in the manufacture of ink, paint and nail polish - the latter as appropriate an antidote to munitions as one could wish for.

As the train slows for STEVENSTON, you catch sight of a graffiti covered concrete abutment, just about all that remains of the Caledonian's Lanarkshire & Ayrshire line to Ardrossan, which bridged the Sou' Western at this point. The L&A had its own station at Stevenston, and whilst stopping passenger services were abandoned as early as 1932 by the LMS who saw no reason to provide two such closely parallel services in the district, the line remained in use until the 1960s for freight and for boat trains to Montgomerie Pier. One of Robert Burns' heroines, Bonnie Lesley ('She's gane, like Alexander, To spread her conquests farther') came from Stevenston.

Although this was once a densely industrialised district, its coastal status also created a demand for leisure, and the railway companies were only too happy to indulge a travelling public anxious for temporary escape from the workaday towns which abounded in its hinterland. The excitement with which these hoards greeted the sea remains palpable as the line runs along the esplanade between Stevenston and Saltcoats. This brief but splendid seaside interlude has been likened by learned sources to Dawlish. And if this shoreline is slightly more austere than its South Devon counterpart, it does have in common continued railway ownership. When the LMS made improvements to the sea defences in 1931, its illustrious Chairman, Sir Josiah Stamp, officiated at the opening ceremony, and the porters at Saltcoats

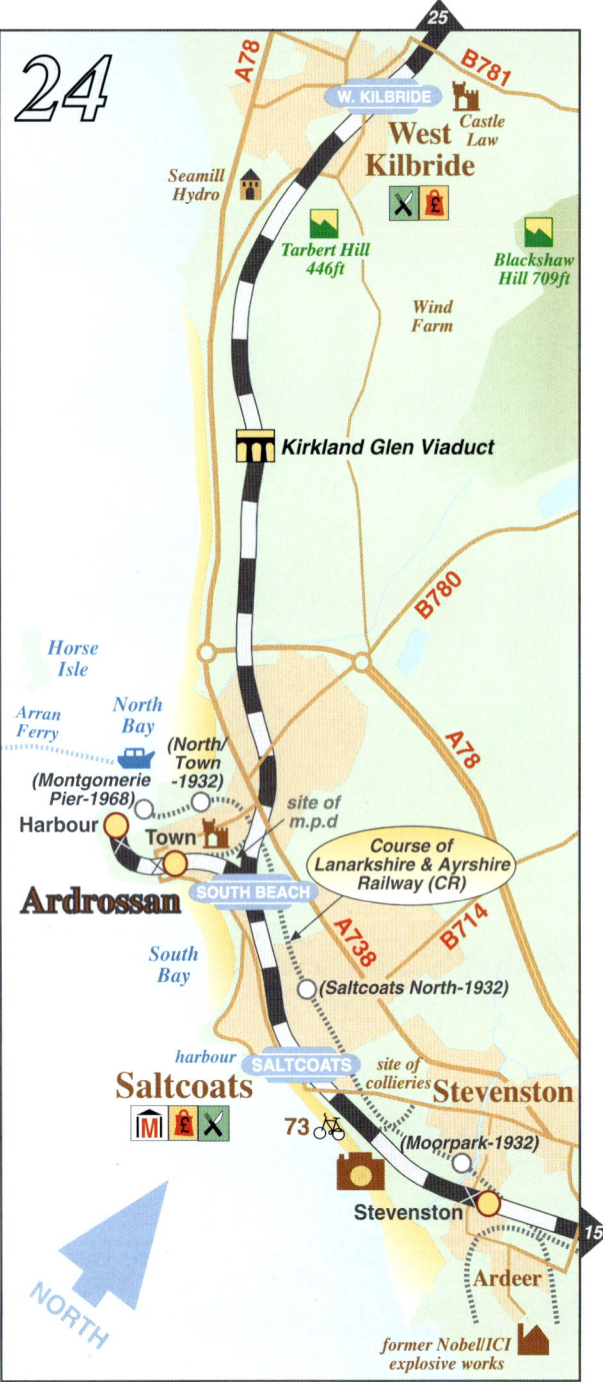

station were issued with new uniforms to mark the event. There are no porters at SALTCOATS now, but at least the booking office remains manned. The red sandstone station buildings are largely intact too, though the main two storey block on the down platform, stolid and rather ugly as it is, could do with being offered a new lease of life, perhaps as an annex to the excellent North Ayrshire Museum which occupies an old church deeper into the town.

Beyond Saltcoats the track remains double, but appearances can be deceptive, for passenger trains are confined to the old down line in both directions; the old up line being used solely by freight trains from Hunterston. ARDROSSAN once boasted no less than five stations. SOUTH BEACH is simply a single platform now (albeit staffed) overlooked by a sward of municpal grass framed by a line of solid villas. Immediately beyond it the line to Town and Harbour stations veers away beneath a hillside bearing one of the ruins 'knocked-about-a-bit' by Cromwell. TOWN station is a disappointing shell of its former self. Two level crossings beyond, HARBOUR is a foreshortened replacement for the G&SWR's Winton Pier terminus. It is as if the Gods are punishing Ardrossan for the hubris of its railway heyday. Wasteground is all that remains where a triangle of lines once embraced a substantial four-road engine shed (27H/30C/67C) which provided motive power for passenger services to Glasgow and Kilmarnock as well as for the huge volume of freight associated with the ICI (nee Nobel) complex at Ardeer. The depot closed to steam in 1965 but remained a stabling point for diesel traction, before becoming a dumping ground for the ill-fated Clayton centre-cab design. Of Ardrossan's other two stations very little trace can be found, a far cry from the days when Montgomerie Pier played host to the Belfast ferry; even further since, prior to completion of the West Coast Main Line, the fastest way of reaching Glasgow from London was by train to Fleetwood and then by boat to Ardrossan, before completing the journey by train to Glasgow.

The line to Largs forges northwards, presenting a curious sight in that one track runs beneath catenary whilst the other doesn't. The electric units of classes 318 and 334 cock a snook at the 1 in 100 climb. In contrast the lengthy trains of empty coal hoppers, hauled by Class 66 locomotives, go growling up the grade. Panoramic views open out across the Firth of Clyde. WEST KILBRIDE, a minor masterpiece by James Miller, deserves better than its current neglect.

Saltcoats Floodtide

53

THE Firth of Clyde disappears behind Goldenberry Hill as the train commences its descent to Largs, like an aeroplane coming in to land. Inland a wind farm is well-sited to make the most of prevailing air currents. In contrast Hunterston's nuclear power stations hove into view. And then, to complete a trilogy of power sources, the terminal responsible for all those heavy coal trains which, one imagines, are assimilated with ever increasing difficulty between the branch's hourly passenger service. All this provides a neat metaphor for the sea change in British industry: the first railways in Ayrshire were built to facilitate the export of coal; the most recent its importation.

The Port of Hunterston dates from as recently as 1979. Initially its chief cargo was imported iron ore, conveyed by rail to Ravenscraig steel works at Motherwell in heavy block trains double-headed by Class 37 diesel locomotives: a dozen Motherwell engines were specially allocated to these duties and given appropriate names. A lengthy pier extended out into the firth to capitalize on its deep water channel, thus enabling the largest of ships to dock. During the Miners' Strike of 1983 imported coal came in through Hunterston - though not for onward carriage by rail because the rail unions were in sympathy with the miners - and this created a precedent for the port's main business now that ore is no longer delivered. Not all the coal which arrives at Hunterston from countries as far away as Australia continues its journey by rail; lorries provide for local distribution, whilst smaller sea-going vessels load here for short haul traffics across the Irish Sea.

Nowadays Hunterston is one of four Clyde ports belonging to a holding company which also owns the Manchester Ship Canal and Liverpool's John Lennon Airport. Plans are being developed to create a deep-water container terminal at Hunterston which, if they came to fruition, would propel Hunterston into the top ten of European ports; a scenario which would have major implications for railfreight. Currently, the coal comes up by conveyor to lineside hoppers at the coal terminal, and the branch down to Hunterston itself is the sole preserve of the occasional DRS operated flask train carrying spent nuclear materials to Sellafield in Cumbria.

'The next stop is Fairlie' the wee Scots lass announces plaintively over the public address system, and when you reach it you can only feel that she has omitted the suffix 'sad';

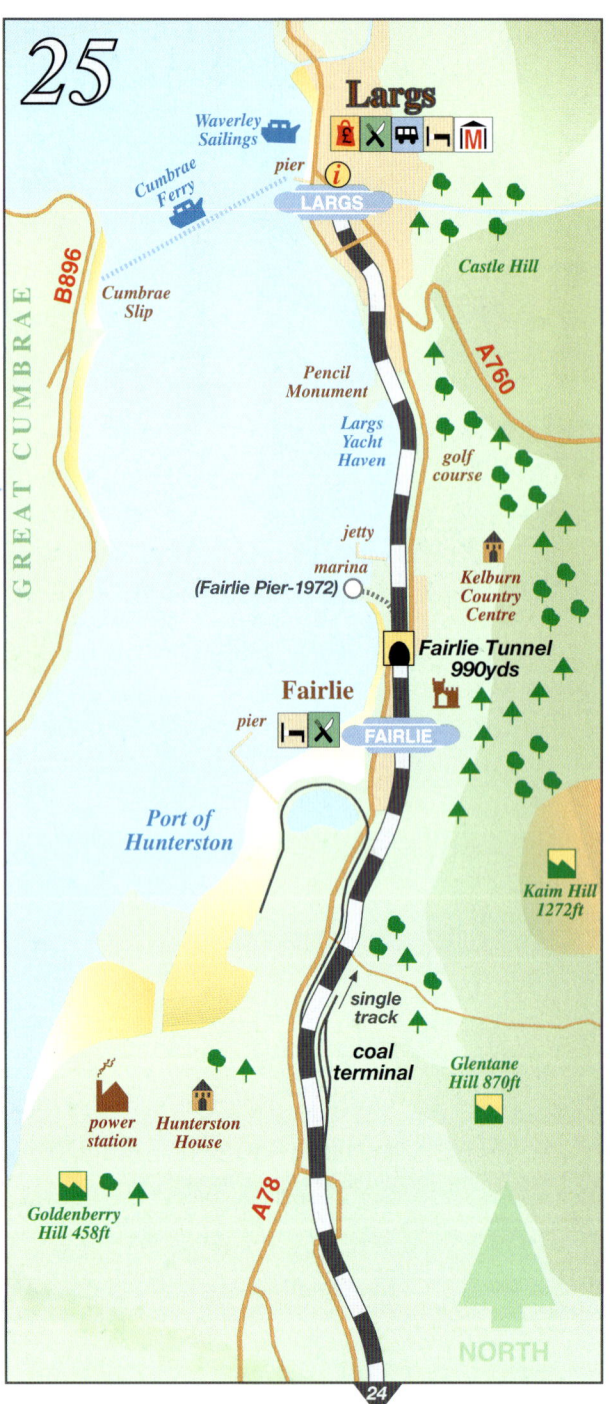

for electrification brought its henchman rationalisation along with it, and where once there stood a pretty timber station building, two platforms linked by a lattice footbridge and a goods-yard with Camping Coaches, now there is just one bare, 'bus-sheltered' platform stretching to the gaping mouth of a dank tunnel.

FAIRLIE PIER station was abandoned in 1972, bringing the curtain down on a picturesque era of boat trains connecting with Clyde steamers: amongst which, at one time, the Glasgow & Sou' Western could claim to operate some of the sleekest and most elegant examples afloat; a fleet characterised by red and black funnels and grey and white hulls. A trio of platforms arced out into the firth, two of them terminating at buffer stops beneath a timber train shed; all very modellable, one imagines, especially given that the layout included a two-road engine shed, home for five years from 1922 to a pair of Robert Whitelegg's Baltic tanks.

'It is improbable that elsewhere in the world today there is any place which has so famously devoted itself to yachting as the Ayrshire village of Fairlie', wrote John Scott Hughes in his *Harbours of the Clyde* (Christopher Johnson 1954). The Fife family were the most famous exponents of yacht building in the neighbourhood, four generations of them who, in the words of their founder, William Fife, were purely concerned with building boats that were 'fast and bonnie'. There is plenty of visual evidence to be gathered through the carriage window that yachting continues to be a preoccupation along this part of the Clyde Coast. Meanwhile, inland lie the gracious purlieus of Kelburn, home to the Earls of Glasgow since the 13th Century, but in these egalitarian times, accessible by the great unwashed as well.

Jointed track ushers you towards the terminus, and you pass the conically-topped 'Pencil' monument commemorating King Alexander III's victory here over King Haakon of Norway in 1263. The last mile emphasises that Largs enjoys residential status commensurate with its well publicised role as a seaside resort. The first train entered LARGS to considerable acclaim in 1885. There were fewer onlookers a hundred and ten years later to witness an electric train fail to stop at the buffers, crash through the booking hall, demolish a pair of shops and come to an undignified halt in Main Street. One can only surmise it had somehow learned of the quality of Nardini's ices, a pilgrimage that you too would be unwise to eschew.

Arran in the Distance

Gazetteer

Annan

The folksinger Kate Rusby has a traditional song in her repertoire called Annan Water, and it is easy to find yourself humming this beautiful air as you perambulate this equally good-looking town and former port on the Solway Firth. Unequivocally Scots, its appearance seems all the more self-defining if you've just arrived from south of the border. The High Street, stretching from the Town Hall to the Old Parish Church encapsulates Annan's inherent dignity, though one senses its glory days are behind it. Annan Bridge, which spans the Nith at the west end of the town, dates from 1824 and is variously attributed to John Rennie or Robert Stevenson circa 1824; the latter being better known for his lighthouses, and for being the grandfather of R.L.S. In 1792 Robert Burns wrote The Deil's Awa' Wi th' Exciseman in what is now the Cafe Royal. The Victorian painter William Ewart Lockhart, whose best known paintings included The Funeral of Burns, also hailed from Annan.

Accommodation

QUEENSBURY ARMS HOTEL - High Street. Tel: 01461 202024 *www.queensberryarmshotel.co.uk* Former coaching inn.

Eating Out

PAGANI'S - High Street. Tel: 01461 201999.

Shopping

The town centre lies less than 5 minutes walk north of the railway station.

Things to Do

ANNAN MUSEUM - Bank Street. Tel: 01461 201384. Local history displays. Open all year round, Mon-Sat, 11am-4pm.

Connections

BUSES - Service 79 operates hourly Mon-Sat and bi-hourly Sun between Carlisle and Dumfries via Annan, providing access to villages such as Eastriggs (for the Devil's Porridge Visitor Centre), Cummertrees (for Powfoot), and Clarencefield (for the Ruthwell Cross) where the railway station closed years ago. Service 383 links Annan with Lockerbie via Ecclefechan, birthplace of Thomas Carlyle.

TAXIS - Macleans. Tel: 01461 202419.

Ardrossan

You are almost two centuries too late to see Ardrossan at its best. As envisaged by the Earl of Eglinton early in the 19th Century, it was to be a port linked by canal to Glasgow. But the lavish Eglinton Tournament of 1839 (Map 15) devoured a good deal of the Earl's fortune and the canal between Ardrossan and Johnstone (Map 13) never materialised. Post-industrially ravaged, Ardrossan is slowly being regenerated, though when contrasted against the expensive yachts in the marina, the poverty of its streets hint at a dichotomy which will take much money and no little imagination to meld.

Accommodation, Eating & Drinking

LAURISTON HOTEL - South Crescent Road. Tel: 01294 463771 *www.lauristonhotel.co.uk* Hotel, restaurant and bar overlooking the front yet within a couple of hundred yards of South Beach station.

Connections

FERRIES - CalMac. Tel: 08705 650000 *www.calmac.co.uk* It takes just a tad under an hour to cross to Brodick on Arran, and having reached Ardrossan it would be remiss of you not to make the voyage, even if you come straight back!

Auchinleck

Railhead now for Cumnock. The colliery on its doorstep has been transformed into a business park. A Tesco supermarket supplies all that civilisation has to offer. Boswell would have made mincemeat of them.

Accommodation

AUCHINLECK HOUSE - 18th Century country house in finely landscaped grounds just over two miles north-west of Auchinleck station. Former home of James Boswell who indulged in much 'social glee' within its neo-Classical walls. Holiday accommodation for up to 13 people. Landmark Trust bookings on 01628 825925 *www.landmarktrust.org.uk*

Connections

BUSES - frequent links with Cummnock. Tel: 0870 608 2 608.
TAXIS - Ten-Ten. Tel: 01290 421010.

Ayr

Ayr celebrated its 800th Anniversary in 2005. It had plenty to crow about, for it is inherently a handsome town, half commercial centre, half seaside resort. Once you have come to terms with this fundamental dichotomy, you can enjoy Ayr for its own sake, turning a blind eye to some of its apparently self-inflicted shortcomings. Architectural highlights include: Loudoun Hall, the 16th Century house of a well to do merchant; the high-spired Town Buildings; the Tudor Gothic folly of the Wallace Tower; the massive County Buildings; and the extraordinarily frivolous seafront Pavilion, erected for dancing in 1911 but now a children's indoor play area. The harbour is worth visiting for its own sake. Here, pubs with names like the Anchor, Steamboat, Ship and Smugglers hark back to an older, wilder version of the town. Between the bustling town centre and the sea lie discreet parcels of Georgian housing. The front has been spruced up in the theme of a Lang Scots Mile - said to be 224 yards lengthier than its English counterpart before the dead hand of uniformity shortened it in the 19th century. And as for the view out to sea, well by then, with a stick of Renaldo's rock clutched tightly in your hand, you will forgive Ayr anything!

Accommodation
STATION HOTEL - Burns Statue Square. Tel: 01292 263268 *www.swallowhotels.com* Now part of the Swallow group and still a joy to stay at for the ancient, hand-worked lift doors alone.
HORIZON HOTEL - The Esplanade. Tel: 01292 264384 *www.horizonhotel.com* Three star hotel on the seafront.
ARRANDALE HOTEL - Cassillis Street. Tel: 01292 289959 *www.arrandalehotel.co.uk* Comfortable accommodation in quiet Georgian street between the town and the seafront.

Eating Out
CAFE MED - Smith Street. Tel: 01291 287193. Gingham table-clothed Greek taverna handily placed across the station forecourt. Bacon rolls, omelettes, pasta, grills and Greek dishes etc.
FOUTERS - Academy Street. Tel: 01292 261391 *www.fouters.co.uk* Fine dining in imaginative basement setting.
TAM O' SHANTER - High Street. Tel: 01292 611684. Cheerful pub with bistro annex, apparently deriving its name from some poem or other.
CECCHINI'S - Fort Street. Tel: 01292 263607 *www.cecchinis.com* Well appointed Italian restaurant which also has a branch at Troon.
THE ROYAL CAFE - New Road. Tel: 01292 263058. Mancini's fish teas and award-winning ice cream parlour established 1913.

Shopping
The town centre is just two minutes walk from the station and Ayr is an important shopping centre for a wide hinterland. There's a bustling Farmers Market on River Street on the 1st Saturday of the month. Elsewhere look out for some endearing specialist outlets such as ROBBIE'S DRAMS (Tel: 01292 262135) who deals in whisky on Sandgate or TRADITIONALLY ARRAN (Tel: 01292 270277) at the station end of High Street for fine foods and creative giftware.

Things to Do
TOURIST INFORMATION - Sandgate. Tel: 0845 22 55 121 *www.ayrshire-arran.com*
PS WAVERLEY - summer season sailings from Ayr Harbour around Ailsa Craig etc. Tel: 0845 130 4647 *www.waverleyexcursions.co.uk*

Connections
TAXIS - Arrow Taxis. Tel: 01292 288288
CAR HIRE - Eurodrive. Tel: 01292 619192 *www.eur.me.uk*

Barrhill
Peaceful village the best part of a mile downhill from its railway station. The Memorial Hall is the work of the ubiquitous James Miller. An engineering works comes as something of a surprise!

Accommodation, Eating & Drinking
KILDONAN COUNTRY HOUSE - holiday apartments and bed & breakfast. Tel: 01465 821360.
THE GALLOWAY HOTEL - Main Street. Tel: 01465 821343. Small hotel, meals for non-residents, locally-caught salmon a speciality.
THE WALLACE ROOMS - Kildonan House. Tel: 01465 821440. Fine dining bar and restaurant.

Shopping
SUZANNE'S STORE - Main Street. Tel: 01465 821235.

Connections
BUSES - links with Girvan and Newton Stewart, one or two of which call at the railway station, the rest run through the village. Tel: 0870 608 2 608.

Carlisle
Despite the Debatable Lands, despite the ebb and flow of border history, Carlisle is culturally, you sense, a city facing firmly south, and as such reminds you forcibly of Shrewsbury in its response to Wales. And yet, as far as this guide is concerned, it makes a fine base camp from which to set off on an exploration of South-west Scotland and its railways. If, on the other hand, you are invading from north of the border - in a distant echo of Bonnie Prince Charlie in 1745, who, if the plaque is to be believed, like his nemesis the Duke of Cumberland, only wanted to shop at Marks & Spencer - make it your business to see the Cathedral, the Castle, Tullie House and the Market Hall.

Accommodation
LAKES COURT HOTEL - Court Square. Tel: 01228 531951 *www.lakescourthotel.co.uk* Comfortably refurbished Victorian hotel handily placed beside the railway station.
IBIS HOTEL - Botchergate. Tel: 01228 518000 *www.ibishotel.com* Travel-lodge style accommodation a few hundred yards from the station.
ANGUS HOTEL - Scotland Road. Tel: 01228 523546 *www.angus-hotel.co.uk* Victorian town house accommodation located to north of River Eden a short taxi ride from the station, see also Almonds Bistro below.

Eating & Drinking
DAVIDS - Warwick Road. Tel: 01228 523578. Fine dining. Tue-Sat lunch and dinner.
RISTORANTE MICHELANGELO - English Damside. Tel: 01228 525117. Italian restaurant underneath the railway arches just north of the station.
ALMONDS BISTRO - Scotland Road. Tel: 01228 523546. Attractive bistro open for dinner Mon-Sat on far bank of Eden.
HOME & AWAY -Tel: 01228 512615. The Crescent. Excellent fish & chips opposite the station.
PRIOR'S KITCHEN - Cathedral Close. Tel: 01228 543251. Crypt located cafe. Closed Sundays.

Shopping
An excellent regional centre for shopping. THE LANES features over seventy big name retailers, but pride of place goes to the COVERED MARKET, a Victorian retailing centre rivalling Citadel station in its architectural splendour. It houses a fine array of stalls, many specialising in Cumbrian delicacies. In Castle Street, BOOKCASE is one of the best secondhand bookshops in the north of England and also specialises in classical music CDs - Tel: 01228 544560. Excellent pies from SPROAT & SON'S bakery at the railway station end of Lowther Street.

Things to Do
CARLISLE VISITOR CENTRE - Old Town Hall. Tel: 01228 625600 *www.historic-carlisle.org.uk*
TULLIE HOUSE MUSEUM & ART GALLERY - Castle Street. Tel: 01228 534781. Award-winning museum devoted to many aspects of Carlisle's fascinating history, not least its railway heyday.
CASTLE - Castle Way. Tel: 01228 591922. Well preserved fortification dating from the 11th Century.
CATHEDRAL - Castle Street. Tel: 01228 548151. 12th Century church built from an attractive shade of red sandstone.

Connections
BUSES - Tel: 0870 608 2 608. Service 79 operates daily from The Courts to Dumfries calling at a number of villages shorn of their railway stations en route. Service 95 leaves the station forecourt on an hourly basis (less frequently on Sundays) for Edinburgh, replicating rail services along the Waverley Route.
TAXIS - City Taxis. Tel: 01228 520000.
CAR HIRE - Europcar, Lancaster Street. Tel: 01228 511760. Friendly and inexpensive car hire, arrangements can be made to collect rail passengers from the station, though their office is less than 5 minutes walk away.

Dumfries
Seagulls provide a perennially jaunty soundtrack to explorations of this rubicund and congenial county town: it is as if they retain some tribal memory of the time when Dumfries was a port whose ships brought tobacco from the colonies. Nowadays a lengthy weir keeps the saltwater at bay and a sequence of bridges preclude navigation, but the Nith continues to provide Dumfries with a focus it would be poorer off without. Above the weir stands Devorguilla's Bridge, solely for pedestrians now, but formerly the main means of crossing the river since it was originally built in the 15th Century. In contrast, downstream, stands an elegant Victorian suspension bridge erected to provide access for the workforce of now vanished tweed mills. Also riverside is Dock Park; as its name implies, the site of the medieval harbour. An apt maritime connection turns on the provision of a monument to two 'Doonhamers' who perished on board the Titanic. Wary of a French invasion, the Royal Dumfries Volunteers drilled here for the first time in 1795, inspiring a memorable toast from Burns: "May we never see the French, nor the French see us." Naturally, echoes of Burns are ubiquitous, but don't swamp Dumfries in the way that a certain English writer can seem to suffocate Stratford-on-Avon. The town's other, less well-known, literary connection is that it was the childhood home of J. M. Barrie, author of *Peter Pan*.

Accommodation

STATION HOTEL - Lovers Walk.Tel: 01387 254316
www.stationhotel.co.uk Former G&SWR hotel refurbished to Best Western standard and literally just across the road from the station.
HAZELDEAN HOUSE - Moffat Road. Tel: 01387 266178
www.hazeldeanhouse.com Quality bed & breakfast accommodation five minutes walk east of the station.
RIVENDELL - Edinburgh Road. Tel: 01387 252251
www.rivendellbnb.co.uk B&B accommodation in attractive Arts & Crafts style house about ten minutes walk east of the station.

Eating & Drinking

STATION CAFE - railway station. Tel: 01387 262605. Light meals, snacks and take-aways from premises on the Carlisle-bound platform.
COURTYARD BISTRO - Station Hotel. Tel: 01387 254316. Evening meals - lunches obtainable in the hotel bar.
THE DOONHAMER - Church Crescent. Tel: 01387 253832
Quintessential Scots cafe open for breakfasts, lunches and teas; plus evening meals Thur, Fri & Sat.
THE GLOBE INN - High Street. Tel: 01387 252335. Burns' drinking 'howff', tucked away in an alley off the High Street. His fling with the barmaid here, Helen Ann Park, resulted in her bearing him a daughter nine days before his wife bore him a son. Bar lunches, admirable though they may be, pale by comparison.

Shopping

The town centre lies a brisk five minutes walk from the station and all likely needs are provided for, if rather underwhelmingly so. A town as characterful as Dumfries should be vying with Castle Douglas in the provision of quality independent shops. Bibliophiles have never really recovered from the closure of JAMES THIN'S bookshop, though BARBOURS department store on Buccleuch Street provides architectural (if not retail) solace.

Things to Do

TOURIST INFORMATION - Whitesands. Tel: 01387 253862.
ROBERT BURNS CENTRE - Mill Road. Tel: 01387 264808.
ROBERT BURNS HOUSE - Burns Street. Tel: 01387 255297.
CAMERA OBSCURA & DUMFRIES MUSEUM - Rotchell Road.
Tel: 01387 253374. Panoramic views and regional history.
THE OLD BRIDGE HOUSE - Mill Road. Tel: 01387 256904. 17th century town house devoted to local history.
DUMFRIES & GALLOWAY AVIATION MUSEUM. Tel: 01387 720487 www.dumfriesaviationmuseum.com Aviation museum housed in former RAF control tower at Heathhall to the east of the town.

Connections

BUSES - service 500/X75 reprises the old 'Port Road' rail link between Dumfries and Stranraer via Castle Douglas and Newton Stewart, and more or less echoes the old two and a half hour schedule; what's more the bus departs from the station forecourt! Tel: 0870 608 2 608.
TAXIS - Radio Taxis.Tel: 01387 255050.
CAR HIRE - GLENRENTAL. Handily placed on the railway station: inexpensive and friendly service. Tel: 01387 266550.

BIKE HIRE - G&G CYCLE CENTRE. Academy Street. Tel: 01387 259483 www.cycle-centre.com

Dunlop

Cattle, cheese, bacon (but not tyres! - that distinction belongs to Dreghorn): Dunlop's gifts are manifold and remarkable in such a small settlement. After a period of absence, the dry, cloth-bound, whole-milk cheese is again being produced in the vicinity by Dunlop Dairy Products - Tel: 01560 482494. Small shop and pub in the village centre.

Fairlie

Fairly exclusive commuter village and boating centre, though lacking the focus now of its erstwhile railway pierhead.

Accommodation, Eating & Drinking

VILLAGE INN - Bay Street. Tel: 01475 568432. CAMRA recommended village pub with rooms and a restaurant (proud of its local produce) called the MUDHOOK after a yachting club formed in 1873.

Girvan

Too self-absorbed to ever become a popular seaside resort, Girvan is an admirable destination for day-trippers attuned to small town atmosphere. The harbour is given colour by its boat repair yard, lifeboat and fishing fleet, whilst iconic Ailsa Craig provides the perfect backdrop for beachcombers.

Accommodation

HOTEL WESTCLIFFE - Louisa Drive. Tel: 01465 712128
www.smoothhound.co.uk Two star hotel on the seafront.

Eating & Drinking

AROMA'S RESTAURANT - Montgomerie Street. Tel: 01465 710071. Open Wed-Sat for lunch and dinner plus Sunday lunch. Emphasis on local produce and freshly caught fish.
HARBOUR CAFE - Knockcushion Street. Tel: 01465 714472. Fish & chips restaurant.
MINERVA CAFE - Bridge Street. Quaintly old-fashioned Scottish cafe. Light meals and knickerbocker glories.

Shopping

A town as yet uncaptured by any of the big supermarket chains. Some nice small shops such as AROMA'S DELICATESSEN on Dalrymple Street and FUNAI'S charming little sweet shop on Knockcushion Street. Some of the best ice creams are to be had from BOB'S ICES on The Flushes.

Things to Do

TOURIST INFORMATION - The Flushes.

Connections

BUSES - services from the railway station to Dailly, Ayr via Turnberry, and Newton Stewart via Pinwherry and Barrhill. Tel: 0870 608 2 608.
TAXIS - Girvan Taxis. Tel: 01465 710000.

Girvan Harbour

Glasgow

Algebraically, if Edinburgh equals Athens, Glasgow equals Chicago. It is a pulsating city peopled by inhabitants characterised by their trenchant wit. But its real strength lies in its Victorian architecture, great vistas of which beckon you onwards from one street to the next. If only the Clyde could be given a more dynamic role, something more satisfying than the pale sad ghosts of the Broomielaw.

Accommodation

QUALITY HOTEL - Gordon Street. Tel: 0141 221 9680
www.choicehotelseurope.com Formerly an illustrious railway-owned hotel providing easy access off the concourse of Central Station.

ARTTO - Hope Street. Tel: 0141 248 2480 www.arttohotel.com
Contemporary yet (by city centre standards) relatively inexpensive accommodation opposite Central Station.

Eating Out

FRANCO'S -Tel: 0141 204 4816. This friendly Italian station concourse cafe/restaurant makes an ideal spot for a quick snack between trains - anything from a cake to a carbonara.

MISS CRANSTONS -Gordon Street. Tel: 0141 204 1122. Tea room and bakers shop within a couple of minutes walk of Central Station.

ROGANO - Exchange Place (Buchanan Street). Tel: 0141 248 4055 www.rogano.co.uk A restaurant, bar and cafe which has been a Glaswegian institution since the 1930s when its Art Deco interior was inspired by the Queen Mary. The main restaurant opens at noon for lunch and again in the evenings for dinner and is both sumptuous and correspondingly expensive. Downstairs, however, the cafe serves food to the same high standards from noon onwards and special low prices apply between 3 and 6pm. The Oyster Bar opens at 11am and is famed for its fish soup, sandwiches and, naturally, its oysters. Rogano is located in an alley to the right of Borders bookshop off Buchanan Street within three minutes walk from Central Station.

Shopping

'The best shopping in the UK outside London'. Miss Cranstons for fresh baking, Marks & Spencers on the station concourse for fresh sandwiches and bottles of wine. Substantial branch of BORDERS bookshop on Buchanan Street open between 8am and 10pm Mon-Sat (10am-9pm Suns) with congenial cafe for bookworms.

Things to Do

TOURIST INFORMATION - George Square. Tel: 0141 204 4400 www.seeglasgow.com

CITY SIGHTSEEING -Tel: 0141 204 0444 www.CitySightseeingGlasgow.co.uk Open top bus tours allowing you to 'hop on and hop off' at over twenty locations. Approximately every 15-20 minutes from outside Central railway station during the summer months. An excellent way to get to know the city.

P.S. WAVERLEY - Tel: 0845 130 4647 www.waverleyexcursions.co.uk Relive the great days of 'doon the watter' tradition.

MUSEUM OF TRANSPORT - Kelvin Hall. Tel: 0141 287 2720 www.glasgowmuseums.com Wonderful celebration of the city's transport history - cars, trams, trains and shipping. Its collection of Pre-Grouping locomotives will particularly appeal to those of a railway bent. Due to move to new riverside premises.

Gretna Green

North of the railway station lies the quaint, touristy, matrimonial village of Gretna Green; south lies the former munitions town of Gretna-not-so-Green: both communities are linked with their shared station by a tarmac footpath.

Accommodation

GRETNA HALL HOTEL -Tel: 01461 338257 www.crerarhotels.com Three star hotel within five minutes walk of the station in Gretna Green - 'a mecca for runaway couples since the 18th century'.

HUNTERS LODGE HOTEL - Tel: 01461 338214 www.hunterslodgehotel.co.uk Voyseyan Arts & Crafts house refurbished as a hotel on the Gretna side of the railway line.

Eating Out

Fish & chips and Chinese takeaway in Gretna; refreshments also available at the Old Blacksmith's and Gateway village - see below.

Shopping

Gift shops galore in Gretna Green, more practical shops in Gretna: post office, bank, pharmacy, Spar, Costcutter, baker & butcher.

GRETNA GATEWAY OUTLET VILLAGE - Tel: 01461 339028 www.gretnagateway.com Thirty-five designer stores, ten minutes walk from the station (unladen!).

Things to Do

OLD BLACKSMITH'S SHOP CENTRE - Gretna Green. Tel: 01461 338441 www.gretnagreen.com The story of Gretna Green's marriage trade.

Connections

BUSES - service 79 links Carlisle with Dumfries via Annan and Gretna calling at villages long ago denuded of their railway stations. Service 382 runs via Lockerbie to Moffat. Tel: 0870 608 2 608.

TAXIS - Gretna Cabs. Tel: 07863 325747.

Irvine

One of the four industrially dysfunctional towns (along with Methil, Linwood and Bathgate) which featured in The Proclaimers seminal song Letter From America. And, typically of Lowland Scotland, a town of contradictions: west of the railway the redundant harbour has been redeveloped with bijou housing and visitor attractions; to the east of the station a lengthy covered shopping mall spans the river and leads to the old core of the town, and some surprisingly handsome architecture.

Accommodation

IRVINE THISTLE HOTEL - Annick Road. Tel: 01294 274272 www.thistlehotels.com Modern 3 Star hotel a short taxi ride from the station.

GAILES HOTEL - Marine Drive, Gailes. Tel: 01294 204040 www.gaileshotel.com Travel lodge style accommodation to south of Irvine by Glasgow Gailes golf course.

Eating & Drinking

MARINA INN - Harbour Street. Tel: 01294 274079. CAMRA recommended bar a few minutes walk west of the station in the redeveloped harbourside area. Belhaven ales and bar food.

Things to Do

SCOTTISH MARITIME MUSEUM - Harbourside. Tel: 01294 278283. Open April to October 10am-5pm daily.

MAGNUM LEISURE CENTRE - Tel: 01294 278381. Leisure multiplex.

VENNEL GALLERY - Tel: 01294 275059. Burns lore, arts and crafts.

EGLINTON COUNTRY PARK - Tel: 01294 551776. '400 hectares of Ayrshire countryside'.

Connections

TAXIS - C Cars. Tel: 01294 271010.

Kilmarnock

Carpets and coal, Tam o' Shanters and trains, whisky and wagonways, Kilmarnock has long been the county's most industrialised centre. History, of course, is perpetually in Kilmarnock's debt, for this was where Burns' poetry was first published by John Wilson in 1786. But that a town of this size is without a tourist information centre in this day and age suggests at best shyness, at worst embarrassment. Yet Kilmarnock should be more confident, for it is a characterful town blessed with many dignified buildings. One need only descend from the haughty railway station directly into the elongated red sandstone vista of John Finnie Street to receive confirmation that Killie has a townscape to contend with - if only they knew it!

Accommodation

THE PARK HOTEL - Tel: 01563 545999 www.theparkhotel.uk.com Smart modern hotel recently established alongside the football stadium, a taxi ride or a gentle walk through appealing suburbs from the station.

Eating & Drinking

CAFE DE VINCI - Strand Street. Tel: 01563 573535. Slick service characterises this atmospheric Italian housed beneath a former whisky bond which lends it the authentic feel of a Naples backstreet.

MAMITA'S - Bank Street. Tel: 01563 573063. Friendly, well furnished coffee bar serving freshly made light lunches etc.

Shopping

The BURNS SHOPPING MALL and King Street play host to many a well known brand name, and it is the diligent shopper who displays patience enough to unearth such delights as D. M. HANNAH & SON, a family grocery established on College Wynd in 1926. 'Killie Pies' from branches of BROWNINGS bakers.

Things to Do

DEAN CASTLE - Tel: 01563 554708. A fortified keep, palace and gatehouse which once belonged to Sir Robert Boyd who fought successfully at Bannockburn. Fine collections of armoury and also musical instruments. The castle and museum are set in a country park with visitor centre and tea room.

THE DICK - museum and art gallery housed in a fine Victorian pile on Elmbank Avenue off London Road, about 10 minutes walk from the station. Tel: 01563 554343.

Connections

BUSES - Tel: 0870 608 2 608. Smartly painted A1 Stagecoach double-deckers ply Kilmarnock's extensive hinterland.

TAXIS - Ten Ten Taxis. Tel: 01563 551010.

CAR HIRE - Arnold Clark. Tel: 01563 541727.

Kilmaurs

There's more to this former weaving village than meets the vacant eye. Dominated by a handsome Tolbooth, its centre plays host to a cafe called GLEG WHITTLE, a butcher called McGARRITY and an excellent cycling shop called WALKERS from which you can hire bikes and peddle off into the Ayrshire countryside - Tel: 01563 544488 www.walkerscycling.co.uk

Kilwinning

Tsunamis of schoolchildren fill Kilwinning's pedestrianised town centre each termtime lunchtime - as indeed they do most Scots towns - and the wise explorer takes care to purchase their luncheon requirements before this invasion takes place. The town is chiefly notable for the remains of its 12th Century Abbey and for its links with the origins of Freemasonry. On its eastern fringe lies EGLINTON COUNTRY PARK (Tel: 01294 551776) which occupies the former demesne of Eglinton Castle, once the grandiose home of the Montgomeries, Earls of Eglinton. A surprisingly vibrant taxi rank at the railway station provides an easy means of reaching the Country Park. A pleasant traffic-free route for walkers and cyclists links Kilwinning with Irvine, four miles to the south.

Kirkconnel

Dour old mining village, justifiably proud of its busier past. Some fine walks to be enjoyed in and around the locality using the railway station as a railhead. Leaflets obtainable from the Heritage Society - see below.

Eating & Drinking
Tea room and fish & chips.

Shopping
Co-op, post office and pharmacy.

Things to Do
KIRKCONNEL PARISH HERITAGE SOCIETY - Main Street. Tel: 01659 66002. Enterprising local history group premises where the public are encouraged to delve into Kirkconnel's history or dig for their roots.

Connections
BUSES - local connections throughout Nithsdale. Tel: 0870 608 2 608.

Largs

Most alluring and vivacious of the Clyde Coast resorts (at least on the mainland!), Largs gains additional appeal as the gateway (by ferry) to the charming town of Millport on Great Cumbrae.

Accommodation
BRISBANE HOUSE HOTEL - Greenock Road. Tel: 01475 687200 www.brisbanehousehotel.com Well appointed hotel on sea front yet within five minutes walk of the station.
NIXONS HOTEL - Barr Crescent. Tel: 01475 673381 www.nixonshotel.com Small 3 Star hotel at northern end of Largs Bay approximately a quarter of an hour's walk from the station.

Eating & Drinking
NARDINI - Main Street. Tel: 01475 689313. Iconic ice-cream maker currently not inhabiting its Art Deco alma mater on the front which, after a ridiculously long impasse, shows promise of being refurbished.
MORRIS'S - Gallowgate Street. Tel: 01475 673352. Popular steak restaurant overlooking the front.

Shopping
Ubiquitious MORRISONS supermarket where the goods yard once stood. Some nice independent shops in the handy town centre.

Things to Do
TOURIST INFORMATION - Main Street. Tel: 01475 676182. This is the local information centre (and very helpful and well equipped it is too) but the Ayrshire & Arran Tourist Board also operate a seasonal information bureau on the railway station.

Connections
FERRY - CALMAC. Tel: 08705 650000 www.calmac.co.uk Ten minute crossings to Cumbrae slip with bus connections to Millport.
BUSES - McGILLS operate coastwise services to/from Largs connecting with the railheads at Wemyss Bay, Gourock and Greenock. Tel: 01475 711122.
TAXIS - BRISBANE TAXIS. Tel: 01475 689990.

Lochwinnoch

It's an intriguing little paradox of history that small industrial communities like this used to despatch day-trippers to the Clyde coast by train. Now, to some extent, the role is reversed and visitors arrive at lately gentrified Lochwinnoch to experience the delights of the nature reserve and country park. Lochwinnoch was once renowned as a centre for furniture making - notably, for the furnishing of TransAtlantic liners such as the *Queen Mary* and *Queen Elizabeth*, *Lusitania* and *Titanic*. At the site of the old loop line station three arched overbridges hint at its former island platform layout. At street level, a bricked-up archway and redundant lamp bracket illustrate the former means of reaching the booking hall.

Eating, Drinking & Accommodation
THE HUNGRY MONK - Tel: 01505 843848. Food (from noon onwards) and comfortable accommodation just two minutes walk east of the station.
BROWN BULL - Main Street. Tel: 01505 843250. CAMRA and Les Routiers recommended former coaching inn.
THE JUNCTION - High Street. Tel: 01505 842225. Cosy bistro in village centre ten minutes walk west of the station.
LA DOLCE VITA - High Street. Tel: 01505 843372. Fish & chips and pizza.
NIXONS@GABLE END - High Street. Tel: 01505 842775. Restaurant in village centre.
CORNER BAR - St Winnoch Road. Tel: 01505 843403. Wee Belhaven howff just a couple of hundred yards from the loop line for thirsty ramblers and cyclists.

Shopping
Post office, convenience stores and delicatessen in village centre.

Things to Do
RSPB RESERVE - Tel: 01505 842663 www.rspb.org.uk/scotland 159 hectares of wetland, wet grassland and woodland adjoining Castle Semple Loch with a visitor centre (open daily throughout the year 10am-5pm) located within a couple of minutes walk of the railway station. Nature trails and birdwatching hides. RSPB shop.

CASTLE SEMPLE CENTRE - Tel: 01505 842882 www.clydemuirshiel.co.uk Regional Park visitor centre (ten minutes walk from the station on a new traffic-free path) offering refreshments and bike and boat hire (see below). Walks to be enjoyed along the lochside and/or the Lochwinnoch Loop Line.

Connections
BUSES - service 307 provides a half-hourly (hourly on Sundays) service linking Lochwinnoch station with Lochwinnoch and the railway stations at Howwood and Johnstone.
BIKE HIRE - Castle Semple Centre. Tel: 01505 842882.
BOAT HIRE - Castle Semple Centre. Tel: 01505 842882.

Maybole

Exiled 'Minniebolers' may well yearn nostalgically for the old capital of Carrick, but it is difficult to imagine it being much of a temptation to tourists. Latent architecture hints at lost dignity; a sadly perfect example of a town overtaken by time.

Eating & Drinking
A handful of cafes and 'carry-outs' strung along the main street.

Shopping
Convenience store handily placed within the old station building; further choice of shops in the town centre 5 minutes walk to the south.

Connections
BUSES - Tel: 0870 608 2 608. Connections to/from Maidens, Dailly and Turnberry.
TAXIS - Hunter's. Tel: 01655 882320.

New Cumnock

Mining community defined by coal board housing schemes at odds with pastoral images of 'sweet' Afton Water. A Town Trail walk leaflet (available from regional TICs) of 4 miles length guides you around left over vestiges of industry. The local football team go by the mellifluous name of Glenafton FC.

Accommodation
LOCHSIDE HOTEL - located on A76 a mile north-west of New Cumnock station. Tel: 01290 333000 www.lochside-hotel.com Well-appointed hotel in prime position between the railway line and the Loch o' th' Lowes. Adjoining golf course.

Paisley

In common with Birkenhead, Sunderland and Wolverhampton, Paisley can appear diminished by the greater city on its doorstep. It compensates, in the manner of all underdogs, by being fiercely proud of its achievements and its alumni: the famously eponymous shawls, sewing threads, cigarettes, shipbuilding (sic), underwear, custard powder, marmalade; the textile barons, the minor poets and architects, religious figures, politicians, singers, actors and even a weather girl. But it is the power of Paisley's architecture

Paisley

Wetherspoon all-day pub housed in former GPO alongside Gilmour Street station.
WEE HOWF - High Street. CAMRA recommended bar at the University end of High Street. Kelburn Brewery ales from Barrhead often available.

Shopping
Alas, ARNOTTS department store (designed by James Maitland in 1924) is boarded up, a victim of our chain store age, of which there is too much evidence in the town centre. By way of an antidote, visit the Farmers Markets, held here on the 2nd and 4th Saturdays in the month.

Things to Do
TOURIST INFORMATION - Gilmour Street. Tel: 0141 889 0711.
MUSEUM & ART GALLERIES - High Street. Tel: 0141 889 3151. Admirable displays of art with a local slant (viz John Byrne of *Tutti Frutti* fame) and of this immensely interesting town's rich history. Good shop dispensing Paisley Pattern wear etc.
PAISLEY ABBEY - Abbey Close. Tel: 0141 889 7654 www.paisleyabbey.org.uk One of Scotland's most celebrated ecclesiastical buildings. King Edward I ordered the destruction of the abbey, but it was rebuilt after Bannockburn. King Robert III lies buried within. It enjoys a fine reputation for its music-making now.
SMA' SHOT COTTAGES - Shuttle Street. Tel: 0141 889 1708 www.smashot.com Open Wednesday and Saturday afternoons, April to September.
THREAD MILL MUSEUM - Mile end Mill, Seedhill Road. Open Wednesday & Saturday afternoons, April to September.

Connections
BUSES - connections to Glasgow Airport and other local towns, notably Barrhead incorporating the route of Tram No.28 with remnants to be seen of the long-abandoned trio of lines between the two towns. Tel: 0870 608 2 608.
TAXIS - Paisley Cab Co. Tel: 0141 887 7770.

Prestwick
Essentially an outer suburb of Ayr ever since trams linked the two in 1901. Nowadays, of course, solely the railway provides an electrified means of public transport between Prestwick and Ayr, the last tram having run in 1931. Sadly, Prestwick has also lost its lido, but golf can always compensate and the beach retains its peerless views of Arran, Ailsa Craig and the Firth of Clyde. Among Prestwick's still rich roll call of interesting buildings are a pair of 18th Century Salt Pan houses and, much in contrast, a former cinema on Main Street designed in 1934 by Alister MacDonald, son of Ramsay the Prime Minister.

Accommodation
NORTH BEACH HOTEL - Links Road. Tel: 01292 479069 www.northbeach.co.uk Small three star hotel overlooking the golf course and within a hundred yards of the railway station.
PARKSTONE HOTEL - Esplanade. Tel: 01292 477286 www.parkstonehotel.co.uk Three star hotel overlooking the seafront within five minutes walk of the station.

Eating & Drinking
STATION CAFE - railway station. Tel: 01292 677985. Open from 6.15am Mon-Sat for light meals and take-aways.
LA FERROVIA DINER - Main Street. Tel: 01292 671998. No obvious railway connection despite the name, but wholesome Italian food and fish & chips in friendly, licenced surroundings.
ELLIOT'S - Main Street. Tel: 01292 677677. Smart bar/restaurant open from 8.30am daily.
RED LION - The Cross. Tel: 01292 470703. Popular pub with wide range of bar food.
THE CAFE - The Cross. Tel: 01292 470597. Daytime restaurant food and home-made Italian ice cream.

Shopping
Wide choice of small shops on Main Street within three minutes walk of the station. Good butcher called HOOD and fine fishmonger called MITCHELL.

Connections
TAXIS - STREAMLINE. Tel: 01292 477525.
BIKE HIRE - PEDALS. Tel: 01292 477455.

Saltcoats
A traditional seaside resort where, despite time's vicissitudes, you can still buy rock, paddle at the water's edge or shelter from the rain in amusement arcades. The be-towered Town Hall presents a picturesque sight from the station.

Eating & Drinking
Clearly not Michelin star territory, but there are bastions of Scots cooking and catering at its wonderfully unhealthy best: there is a fine fish & chip bar adjoining the Glasgow-bound platform at the railway station; in the town centre look out for the KANDY BAR bakery and coffee bar (established 1929) on Hamilton Street; ditto Wetherspoon's SALT COT. At the Ardrossan end of Hamilton Street stands CAVANI'S ice cream emporium (established 1902) which sells its own Italian recipe as well as local rock. VINCENTS, in Windmill Street, is a fish & chip shop with a restaurant section.

Shopping
Most of life's more mundane essentials within a minute or two's walk of the station.

Things to Do
NORTH AYRSHIRE MUSEUM - Tel: 01294 464174. Recently refurbished exhibitions of local history in former parish church.

Connections
TAXIS - Central Taxis. Tel: 01294 464646.

Sanquhar
Post-industrial township in Covenanter country, the manufacture of school furniture being its mainstay now in place of blankets, bricks, shovels, spades and coal. The unusual name derives from the ancient fort of Sean Caer. Also known for its traditional hand-knitting of distinctive black and white pattern.

which most strikes the perceptive visitor now, a hugely rewarding legacy of late Victorian and Edwardian town and public buildings. Put off the coast 'til tomorrow, spend a day in Paisley!

Accommodation
WATERMILL HOTEL - Lonend. Tel: 0141 889 3201 www.thewatermillhotel.co.uk Comfortably refurbished hotel based in former mill beside the White Cart Water.

Eating & Drinking
CARDOSI'S - Storie Street. Tel: 0141 889 5720. New York/Italian restaurant named after one of Paisley's famous Italian ice cream makers.
STONES - Canal Street. Tel: 0141 889 3693. Bar/grill housed in former Paisley Canal station buildings.
THE LAST POST - County Square. Tel: 0141 849 6911.

Accommodation
BLACKADDIE HOUSE HOTEL - Blackaddie Road. Tel: 01659 50270 www.blackaddiehotel.co.uk Comfortable country house hotel on edge of town.

Eating & Drinking
A couple of inns and a couple of ethnic take-aways.

Shopping
The Post Office, dating from 1712, lays claim to being the oldest in regular use in the world. For neighbours it boasts a butcher, baker, pharmacy and newsagent, along with SPAR, MACE and CO-OP stores.

Things to Do
TOLBOOTH MUSEUM - High Street. Tel: 01659 50186. Open April to September 10am-1pm and 2pm-5pm Tue-Sat and 2pm-5pm Sun. Admission free. Excellent museum of Sanquhar's colourful history housed in handsome 18th Century building.

Connections
BUSES - Service 246 links Sanquhar daily at fairly regular intervals with Dumfries via Thornhill and Ayr via Cumnock. Service 30 operates Mon-Sat across the grain of the countryside to Wanlockhead (with its lead mine and narrow gauge railway) and Lanark where there are rail connections to Glasgow via Motherwell. Tel: 0870 608 2 608.
TAXIS - Grierson's. Tel: 01659 67000.

Stewarton
Sherpa Tensing was wearing a balaclava knitted in Stewarton when he scaled Everest with Edmund Hillary, and they still 'knit weel' in 'bonnet toun' as well as also engaging in other more cutting edge industries such as the manufacture of wind turbines. The station is central for the shops (butchers, bakers and a greengrocer) an excellent fish & chip bar and an Italian ice cream parlour - what more might you ask for!

Stranraer
The old capital of Wigtownshire will have to re-invent itself when the Belfast ferry ups anchor to Cairnryan. But perhaps this will prove a blessing in disguise, ferry ports are by definition simply places for passing through, turnstiles to somewhere else, made dowdy by the wear and tear of travellers. And Stranraer holds a trump card in the splendour of its setting at the head of Loch Ryan. A bit of a makeover, a reduction in the traffic which inexplicably fills its thoroughfares, and, if it plays its cards right, a whole new generation of tourists will be tempted to visit it for its own sake. One only has to walk along the rim of the sea loch as sunset casts its rays over Ailsa Craig and Arran to experience the latent magic of the town. Whilst, once the ferries have gone, more can be made of the harbour for leisure, with boating positively encouraged.

Accommodation
NORTH WEST CASTLE HOTEL - Port Rodie. Tel: 01776 704413 www.mcmillanhotels.com Former home of the Arctic explorer Sir

Stranraer

John Ross long since established as Stranraer's premier (and friendly with it) hotel, featuring not only its own swimming pool but also an indoor curling rink! Located directly alongside the railway station. Excellent dining with piano accompaniment open to non-residents.
LAKEVIEW GUEST HOUSE - Agnew Crescent. Well-appointed accommodation in harbourside house overlooking Loch Ryan within 5 minutes walk of the railway station.

Eating & Drinking
L'APPERITIF - London Road. Tel: 01776 702991. The cooking is of Italian origin rather than the French insinuated by the name, yet (with the exception of the North West Castle's Regency Dining Room) this is Stranraer's most sophisticated restaurant open Mon-Sat for lunch and dinner; booking essential.
STAR FISH RESTAURANT - Charlotte Street. Tel: 01776 707235.

Town centre cafe offering fish teas for a fiver, pot of tea and bread & butter inclusive!
THE ARCHES - Hanover Street. Tel: 01776 702196. Family restaurant. Great breakfasts!

Shopping
Despite the existence of a large Morrisons and a small Tesco, Stranraer still hosts its fair share of independent retailers of the ilk of JOHN GILLESPIE & SONS, a nice old-fashioned Scots bakery on Castle Street with some wonderful shop-fittings from a past era on display, and FRASER'S, a butcher's shop on Hanover Street with a fine array of pies and haggis in the window.

Things to Do
TOURIST INFORMATION - Harbour Street. Tel: 01776 702595.
STRANRAER MUSEUIM - George Street. Tel: 01776 705088. Excellent displays of local history and happenings open Mon-Sat all year round, admission free.
CASTLE OF ST JOHN - Charlotte Street. Tel: 01776 705544. Medieval tower house dating from circa 1500. Open Mon-Sat, Easter to mid-September, admission free. Incongruous in its setting amongst modern-day shops and cafes, yet great swashbuckling fun for children of all ages. Great views from the top of the tower.
AGNEW PARK -seafront gardens with miniature railway and poignant memorial to the Princess Victoria which foundered in 1953.

Connections
BUSES - service 500 runs via Newton Stewart and Castle Douglas to Dumfries railway station, shadowing the course of the old 'Port Road' railway, and suggesting the possibility of a round trip. There are also local connections with the picturesque old town of Portpatrick. Tel: 0870 608 2 608.
TAXIS - McLean's Taxis. Tel: 01776 703343.
CAR HIRE - G. K. Group. Tel: 01776 703443.
FERRY - Stena Line. Tel: 08705 707070 www.bookstenaline.com Inexpensive day trips to Belfast - 1hr 45mins from Stranraer. Interesting range of coach trip add-ons to various visitor attractions in Ulster.

Troon
James Miller returned to the scene of his triumphant station forty years on and designed Troon's Town Hall. They advertise Tea Dances in it now, which speaks volumes with regard to the extramural activities of Troon's superannuated golfers. But there is more to Troon than genteel atrophy. It has re-invented itself, for example, as a ferry port for Ulster (a role which challenges Stranraer's historic supremacy), whilst in place of colliers its harbour - designed by William Jessop for the Duke of Portland and for many years railway-owned - is now the haunt of expensive-looking yachts. Furthermore, wide firm sands face both bays and offer fine views out to the bird sanctuary of Lady Isle.

Accommodation
THE MARINE HOTEL - Crosbie Road. Tel: 01292 314444 www.paramount-hotels.co.uk/marine Deluxe golfing hotel.